from
SOUND
to
SENTENCE

Learning to Read and *Write* English

Raymond C. Clark

Illustrations by Len Shalansky

PRO LINGUA  ASSOCIATES

Pro Lingua Associates, Publishers
P.O. Box 1348
Brattleboro, Vermont 05302 USA
Office: 802-257-7779
Orders: 800-366- 4775
Email: info@ProLinguaAssociates.com
WebStore www.ProLinguaAssociates.com
SAN: 216-0579

At Pro Lingua
our objective is to foster an approach
to learning and teaching that we call
interplay, the interaction of language learners
and teachers with their materials,
with the language and culture,
and with each other in active, creative
and productive play.

Copyright © 2007 by Raymond C. Clark
ISBN 0-86647-251-7

The author of the poem "The Craziest Language" on page 146 is unknown.
The information and events in Review 3 are based on the following sources:
    US Cities: *Time Almanac*, 2006
    Community Events: the Town of Brattleboro, VT, and the *Brattleboro* (VT) *Reformer*.
    Food Festivals: www.randmcnally.com, www.americanprofile.com/happenings, and various Web sites.

This book was designed by Susannah Clark using Verdana, Gill Sans, and Times New Roman. The cover was designed by Arthur A. Burrows. Printed and bound by McNaughton and Gunn of Saline, MI.

Printed in the United States of America
Second printing 2009. 2,000 copies in print.

CONTENTS

SOUNDS – LETTERS – WORDS – SENTENCES
NUMBERS – DIRECTIONS *(CD 1: track 1)* v

UNIT 1 • **A E I P B T D** *(CD 1: tracks 2–4)* 1
- yes – and - no
  I – you – he – she – it – we – they – am – are – is
- 0 – 1 – 2 – 3 – 4 – 5

UNIT 2 • **S ST** *(CD 1: tracks 5–7)* 13
- **H** but, a, the, that, this, mother, brother, father, sister, daughter, son
- 6 – 7 – 8 – 9 – 10

UNIT 3 • **O M N SS SP SN** *(CD 1: tracks 8–10)* 25
- **W** – WH questions – here – there – everywhere
- 11 – 12 – 13 – 14 – 15

UNIT 4 • **U L R BL PL SL BR DR PR** *(CD 1: tracks 11–13)* 37
- do – does – don't – doesn't – did – didn't – done
  have – has – haven't – hasn't – had
- 16 – 17 – 18 – 19 – 20 – plus

UNIT 5 • **-ED -ER TH** *(CD 2: tracks 1–3)* 48
- to – of – from – or – for – on – off – these – those
- 30 – 40 – 50 – 60 – 70 – 80 – 90

REVIEW 1 *(CD 2: track 4)* 60

UNIT 6 • **C K G CK CL CR GL GR** *(CD 2: tracks 5–7)* 64
- **NK NG TH**
- 100 – 1,000 – 1,000,000

UNIT 7 • **H SH CH TCH A..E AY AI** *(CD 2: tracks 8–9)* 73
- me – my – you – your – him – his – her – it – its – us – our – them – their
  Sunday – Monday – Tuesday – Wednesday – Thursday – Friday – Saturday

UNIT 8 • **E EE EA Y I..E IE IGH** *(CD 2: tracks 10–11)* 83
- mine – yours – his – hers – ours – theirs
- **-'LL -LE** – word stress: **LIS**ten – re**VIEW**
- *A a B b C c D d E e*

UNIT 9 • **C EI F V FL FR O** (*CD 3: tracks 1–2*) 94
   • **EY**
   • word stress: **CON**sonant – Sep**TEM**ber
   • **EA – TI**
   • word stress: **AC**tion cor**REC**tion compre**HEN**sion
   • *Ff Gg Rr*

REVIEW 2 105

UNIT 10 • **O OW O..E OA OR AU A AW AR OU O** (*CD 3: tracks 3–4*) 109
   • **KN** silent **H** silent **B**
   • **W** and **Y** as consonants
   • *Hh Ii Ll Ss*

UNIT 11 • **J G DG U OO UE U..E EW** (*CD 3: tracks 5–6*) 117
   • **WR TW TR** (y)**U**
   • January – February – March – April – May – June – July – August –
      September – October – November – December
   • *Jj Kk Oo Tt*

UNIT 12 • **QU SQU OW OU** (*CD 3: tracks 7–8*) 126
   • **SK SC SCR GH**
   • *Mm Nn Pp Uu*

UNIT 13 • **OY OI IR ER OR UR AR** (*CD 3: tracks 9–11*) 133
   • **PH** (h)**WH**
   • **SPR STR SW SM SPL**
   • point – zero – equal – Fahrenheit – Celsius – percent – centimeter –
      kilometer – inch – mile
   • *Qq Vv Ww*

UNIT 14 • **X Z ZZ** (*CD 3: track 12*) 142
   • The Craziest Language
   • *Xx Yy Zz*

REVIEW 3 • U.S. Cities – Events – Festivals 148

DICTIONS 156

COMMON SOUNDS AND SPELLINGS 162

Oh?

EEEEEEEE

AAAAH

Ay YAY AY YAY AY

MMMMMM

ZZZZZZZ

SHHHH

BRRRRR

HISSSSSSSS

QUACK

A E I O U

S R T N L

M G D B P

C Y H W F

K V X Q J Z

I am learning to read English.

I am learning to write English.

I am learning to read and write English.

MY NAME IS _____ _____.

MY PHONE NUMBER IS _____.

I LIVE AT _____.

MY TEACHER IS _____ _____.

1	ONE	11	ELEVEN
2	TWO	12	TWELVE
3	THREE	13	THIRTEEN
4	FOUR	14	FOURTEEN
5	FIVE	15	FIFTEEN
6	SIX	16	SIXTEEN
7	SEVEN	17	SEVENTEEN
8	EIGHT	18	EIGHTEEN
9	NINE	19	NINETEEN
10	TEN	20	TWENTY

30	THIRTY	70	SEVENTY
40	FORTY	80	EIGHTY
50	FIFTY	90	NINETY
60	SIXTY	100	A HUNDRED

1,000 A THOUSAND

1,000,000 A MILLION

LOOK   LISTEN   SAY

READ   WRITE

ASK   ANSWER   SPELL

2 + 2

AND

A E I B P D T

SOUND-LETTER WORK 1.1 • SOUNDS • LOOK, LISTEN, AND SAY

	A	E	I
B	AB	EB	IB
	BA	BE	BI
	BAB	BEB	BIB
P	AP	EP	IP
	PA	PE	PI
	PAP	PEP	PIP
D	AD	ED	ID
	DA	DE	DI
	DAD	DED	DID
T	AT	ET	IT
	TA	TE	TI
	TAT	TET	TIT

SOUND-LETTER WORK 1.2 • WORDS • LOOK, LISTEN, AND SAY

PAT	PET	PIT
BAT	BET	BIT
PAP	PEP	PIP
BAD	BED	BID
TAP	PED	DIP
PAD	DEB	TIP
DAD	TED	BIB
TAB	TET	DID

SOUND-LETTER WORK 1.3 • READ AND SAY

DAD	PAT	DEB
TED	BED	DID
BAT	BIB	BET
TIP	PAD	BAD
PEP	TIP	PET
PIT	TAP	BID

SOUND-LETTER WORK 1.4 • LOOK

A = a   E = e   I = i

B = b   P = p   D = d   T = t

SOUND-LETTER WORK 1.5 • SOUNDS • LOOK, LISTEN, AND SAY

	b	p	d	t
	b	p	d	t
a	ab	ap	ad	at
	bab	pap	dad	tat
e	eb	ep	ed	et
	beb	pep	ded	tet
i	ib	ip	id	it
	bib	pip	did	tit

SOUND-LETTER WORK 1.6 • WORDS • READ AND SAY

it	ad	Ed	id	at	bed
tap	Ted	dab	dip	pad	Pat
tip	tab	bib	did	Dad	bid
pit	bet	tat	pet	Deb	bit
bat	pap	pep	pip	tet	bad

Dad   Ted   Pat   Deb   Ed

Ed did it?

Dad did it?

Ted did it?

Pat did it?

Deb did it.

SOUND-LETTER WORK 1.8 • WRITE

A A A A A

E E E E E

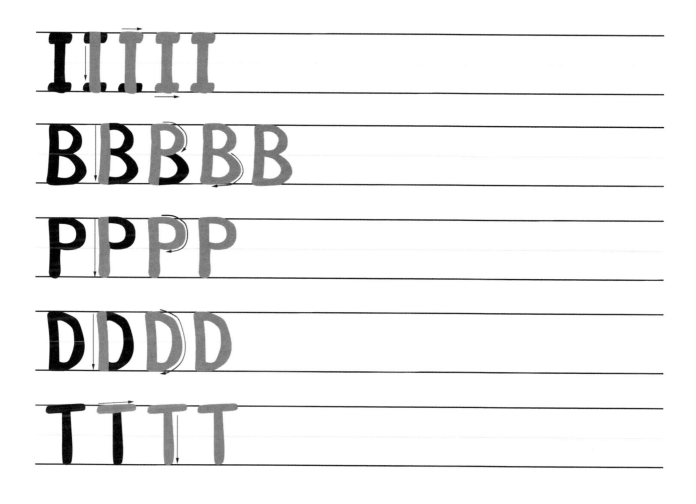

I I I I I

B B B B B

P P P P

D D D D

T T T T

a = a

a a a a

e e e e

i i i i

b b b b

p p p p

d d d d

t t t t

? ? ? ?

Ed did it? _____

Dad did it? _____

Ted did it? _____

Pat did it? _____

Deb did it. _____

_____ _____ _____

_____ _____ _____

_____ _____ _____

_____ _____ _____

🔘 **SOUND-LETTER WORK 1.12 • LOOK AND LISTEN**

THE ALPHABET

A B C D E F G H I J K L M N O P Q R S T U V W X Y Z

a b c d e f g h i j k l m n o p q r s t u v w x y z

🔘 **SOUND-LETTER WORK 1.13 • LISTEN AND SAY**

A a	E e	I i
B b	**P p** **D d**	**T t**
b - a - b	p - a - p	d - a - d
t - a - t	b - e - t	b - e - d
p - e - d	t - e - d	d - i - p
p - i - t	d - i - d	t - i - e

_____   _____   _____

_____   _____   _____

_____   _____   _____

SOUND-LETTER WORK 1.15 • SPELL (SAY)

ad	bad	bat	Pat
Ed	bed	pet	bet
pip	bit	pit	dip
Deb	pad	bet	Ted

WORD WORK 1.1 • LOOK

Y = y   N = n   S = s   O = o

WORD WORK 1.2 • LOOK, LISTEN, AND SAY

YES   AND   NO

YES, YES, YES!   NO, NO, NO!

YES AND NO

yes   and   no

Yes, yes, yes!   No, no, no!

Yes and no.

Dad did it? No, Deb did it.

Deb did it? Yes, Deb did it.

Pat and Deb did it? No, no, no! Deb did it.

Ed and Ted did it? No, no, no! Deb did it.

So, Deb did it. Yes, yes, yes! Deb did it.

WORD WORK 1.3 • READ AND SAY

Pat and Deb did it. No, Dad and Ed did it.
Pat did it? No, Dad did it.
Deb did it? No, Ed did it.
Dad did it? Yes, Dad and Ed did it.
Ed did it? Yes, Ed and Dad did it.

WORD WORK 1.4 • LOOK

$$M = m \qquad R = r \qquad W = w \qquad U = u$$

$$H = h \qquad TH = th \qquad SH = sh$$

WORD WORK 1.5 • LOOK, LISTEN, AND SAY

I AM	YOU ARE	HE IS	SHE IS	IT IS
	WE ARE		THEY ARE	
I am	you are	he is	she is	it is
	we are		they are	
Am I?	Are you?	Is he?	Is she?	Is it?
	Are we?		Are they?	

Are you? Yes, I am. Is he? No, she is. Are we? Yes we are.

Are they? No, we are.

I am Pat.

You are Ted.

He is Ed.

She is Deb.

We are Pat and Ed.

They are Ed and Deb.

WORD WORK 1.7 • READ

Are you Pat and Ted?   Yes, we are.
Are they Ed and Deb?   Yes they are.
Are you Ed?   No, I am Ted.
Is she Deb?   Yes, she is Deb.
Is he Ted?   No, he is Ed.

NUMBER WORK 1.1 • LOOK, LISTEN, AND SAY

0	1	2	3	4	5
5	4	3	2	1	0
1	3	5	2	4	0
2	4	0	3	5	1
B1	T3	D2	P4	E5	I2
A3	P5	D4	E1	3D	2A
1E	4B	5A	15	24	03

NUMBER WORK 1.2 • READ AND SAY

321	512	250	342	314	450
2134	5324	1534	2153	4215	0310

254-3412   321-4523   413-5351   502-4103

125-413-2212   313-454-5352   402-145-3031

NUMBER WORK 1.3 • WRITE

0 0 0

1 1 1 1 1

2 2 2 2

3 3 3 3

4 4 4 4 4

5 5 5 5 5

_____ _____ _____ _____ _____ _____

_____ _____ _____ _____ _____ _____

_____ _____ _____

_____ - _____ - _____ -

_____ - _____ - _____ -

_____ - _____ _____ - _____

NUMBER WORK 1.5 • LOOK

F = f   V = v

0 = OH   1 = ONE   2 = TWO

3 = THREE   4 = FOUR   5 = FIVE

UNIT 2 **S ST**

SOUND-LETTER WORK 2.1 • SOUNDS • LOOK, LISTEN, AND SAY

S s

sa	se	si

its	ats	ets	ips	aps	eps
sat	set	sit	sap	sep	sip

S s

as	es	is

ids	ads	eds	ibs	abs	ebs
sabs	sebs	sibs	sads	seds	Sids

SOUND-LETTER WORK 2.2 • WORDS • READ AND SAY

sit	at	it	set	sits
sip	sap	pats	pets	pits
bad	sad	Sid	dad	pad
as	is	bibs	peds	dads
pads	sips	saps	ads	abs
TABS	BEDS	SITS	SIPS	DADS

It is Pat's bat.
Pat's bat is a pet.

It's Sid.   Sid is Pat's dad.

Is Sid Ed's dad? Yes, Ed's dad is Sid.
Sid is Pat and Ed's dad. Ted and Deb's dad is Sid.

SOUND-LETTER WORK 2.4 • LOOK, LISTEN, AND SAY

ST   st

stap	step	stip	past	pest	pist
stab	steb	stib	bast	best	bist
stat	stet	stit	tast	test	tist
stad	sted	stid	dast	dest	dist

STOP   =   Stop!

SOUND-LETTER WORK 2.5 • READ AND SAY

step	stab	stat	stet	past
pest	best	test	steps	stabs
stats	pests	stet	tests	step
STAT	TEST	STET	PAST	BEST

SOUND-LETTER WORK 2.6 • READ

Sid	bat	pest	pets	sit	step
test	best	Pat's pet bat	pest	Pip	stabs

Pip is Pat's pet bat. Pip bit Pat's dad. Pat is sad. Pip is bad. Pip is a pest.

Ed steps on Pip, Pat's pet bat.

Deb's test is best.

S S S

s s s

ST ST

st st

! ! ! !

pest _____	best _____	steps_____
pets _____	tests _____	bats _____
Ed's _____	beds _____	ads _____
stabs_____	Deb's _____	Pat's _____

Pat's pet _____ Pat's bat _____

It's Sid. _____ Pat's dad_____

Stop! _____ Stop it, Ed! _____

Is it a test? Yes, _____ .

Is Sid Ed's dad? Yes, _____ .

Is Pip Pat's pet? Yes, _____ .

Is it a pest? Yes, _____ .

SOUND-LETTER WORK 2.9 • LISTEN AND WRITE

_____   _____   _____

_____   _____   _____

_____   _____   _____

_____   _____   _____

SOUND-LETTER WORK 2.10 • LISTEN AND SAY

S s

S-T   s-t   a-d-s   b-e-d-s   s-t-e-p   s-t-a-b

p-e-s-t   b-e-s-t   s-i-t-s   t-e-s-t-s   p-a-s-t-e   p-i-t-s

SOUND-LETTER WORK 2.11 • LISTEN AND WRITE

_____   _____   _____

_____   _____   _____

_____   _____   _____

SOUND-LETTER WORK 2.12 • SPELL

beds	best	step	sips	past
stab	ads	test	pests	sits

WORD WORK 2.1 • LOOK, LISTEN, AND SAY

but   a   the   that   this

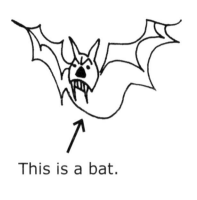

This is a bat.

That is a bat.

A bat is a bad pet.

This bat is Pat's pet.
Pat's pet is bad.
The pet bit Sid.
Pat's pet is a pest.
Is it a bad pet?

WORD WORK 2.3 • LOOK, LISTEN, AND SAY

mother   brother   other   another

one   son

father   sister   daughter

BUT: Beth

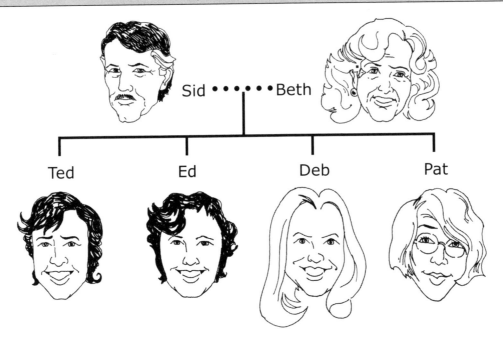

Sid ● ● ● ● ● ● Beth

Ted   Ed   Deb   Pat

Sid Epson is the father. Beth Epson is the mother. Pat and Deb are the daughters. Ted and Ed are the sons. Sid is Ed's father. Ted is Ed's brother. Pat is Deb's sister. Ted is Sid's son. Ed is another son. Deb is Beth and Sid's daughter. Ted and Ed and Pat and Deb's mother is Beth. They are the Epsons.

WORD WORK 2.5 • WRITE

H H H H H

h h h h

the _____   this _____   that _____

Is it a pet? Yes, _____ .

Is it a bat? Yes, _____ .

Is this a bad pet? Yes, _____ .

Is this a bed? Yes, _____ .

Is Ed in the bed? Yes, _____ .

Is that Ed Epson? Yes, _____ .

Is it the best bed? Yes, _____ .

0	1	2	3	4	5
6	7	8	9	10	0
10	9	8	7	6	5
4	3	2	1	0	00
B6	T9	D8	P7	E10	I9
A7	P6	D10	E8	8D	7A
6E	9B	I-10	9S	T7	10S

NUMBER WORK 2.2 • READ AND SAY

9	10	7	8	6	10
7B	9A	10E	SP8	T6D	I-10
976	871	769	386	375	996
2958	5867	8694	6078	4219	7843

808-6779　　321-9966　　478-5351　　902-8706

165-493-8812　　373-484-6602　　482-175-7731

6 6 6

7 7 7 7

8 8 8

9 9 9 9

10 10

NUMBER WORK 2.4 • LISTEN AND WRITE

0 = OH = oh   1 = ONE = one

2 = TWO = two   3 = THREE = three

4 = FOUR = four   5 = FIVE = five

X = x   G = g

6 = SIX = six   7 = SEVEN = seven

8 = EIGHT = eight   9 = NINE = nine

O M N SS SP SN

 SOUND-LETTER WORK 3.1 • LOOK, LISTEN, AND SAY

O o

Bob	bop	bot	bod	boss
pop		pot	pod	poss
top		tot		toss
dot		Dot		dos
sob	sop	sot	sod	stop
pots	tops	Bob's	spot	spots

SOUND-LETTER WORK 3.2 • READ AND SAY

Bob	Dot	pot	spot	boss
top	stop	toss	bop	pop
tot	sob	spots	tops	

SOUND-LETTER WORK 3.3A • READ

a pot

a top

a dot

a spot

pop

stop

A tot sobs.

Bob is at Dot's spot.

Dot is Bob's boss.
She's the boss.

SOUND-LETTER WORK 3.4 • LOOK, LISTEN, AND SAY

M m

mad	mass	mess	miss	moss
met	mid	mob	mop	mat
map	med	mod	mom	

Pam   Sam   Tim   Tom

dam   dim   bam

stem   spam

am

SOUND-LETTER WORK 3.5 • READ AND SAY

Pam	Tim	Dot	Tom	Sam	Bob
boss	map	dam	met	mad	pop
pot	spot	mass	dim	mop	miss
toss	dot	spam	mob	moss	mat
mess	toss	dot	sob	stop	

SOUND-LETTER WORK 3.6 • READ

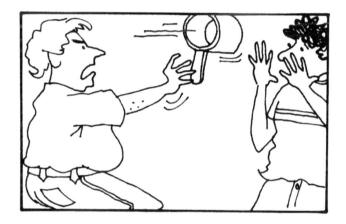

Bob's boss is Dot. Dot is Tom's mom. Bob's boss is mad at Tom. Dot is mad at Tom and Bob. Dot's spot is a mess. Tom tossed a pot at Bob. Bob tossed the mop at Tom. Tom's boss is mad.

N n

an	in	on
nab	neb	nib	nob
nap	nep	nip	nop
pan	pen	pin	pon

and   end   sand   ant   send   sent

snip   snap   snob   spin   span

Ann

SOUND-LETTER WORK 3.8 • READ AND SAY

pan   Don   pin   den   bond   Ben   men   man   on   band

tin   ten   ban   sent   din   stand   and   Dan   pond   Ann   Pam

SOUND-LETTER WORK 3.9 • READ

Dan and Ben met Don, Ann, and Pam at the pond. Don is in the pond.
Pam is on the sand. Pam sits, and Ann and another man stand on the
sand.

O O O

o o o

M M M M M M

m m m m m

N N N N N

n n n n

Ben, Nan, and Tom _____

Mom and Pop _____

Pam's on the sand. _____

Don's in the pond. _____

SOUND-LETTER WORK 3.11 • LISTEN AND WRITE

1 _____   2 _____   3 _____   4 _____

5 _____   6 _____   7 _____   8 _____

9 _____   10 _____

SOUND-LETTER WORK 3.12 • LISTEN AND SAY

A E I B P D T S

O o   M m   N n

B-o-b	D-o-t	T-o-m
P-a-m	D-o-n	A-n-n
m-o-p	t-i-n	p-e-n
m-e-s-s	s-e-n-d	m-i-s-s

SOUND-LETTER WORK 3.13 • LISTEN AND WRITE

1 _____   2 _____   3 _____

4 _____   5 _____   6 _____

7 _____   8 _____   9 _____

SOUND-LETTER WORK 3.14 • SPELL (SAY)

mad	Ben	mom	Tim	mod	spot
pond	mess	sand	spin	boss	stand

WORD WORK 3.1 • LOOK, LISTEN, AND SAY

WHAT   WHEN   WHERE   WHY   WHICH

WHO   WHOSE   HOW

WORD WORK 3.2 • READ AND SAY

Where is Tom?	He's at Dot's.
Who is Dot?	She's Bob's boss.
How is Tom?	He's sad.
Why is Tom sad?	Dot's mad at Tom.
Who's at the pond?	Don and Pam.
Which one is in the pond?	Don is.
What is Pat's pet?	It's a bat.
Whose bat is that?	That's Pat's.

WORD WORK 3.3 • LOOK, LISTEN, AND SAY

HERE   THERE   EVERYWHERE

Where's Pat's bat?	It's everywhere!
Everywhere?	It's here. It's there.
Where?	Here and there.
Ah! Everywhere!	Yes, here, there, everywhere.

Where are Dan and Ben?
Where?
Where are Don and Pam?
Where?
Are there others at the pond?
Is there a bat at the pond?
Whose bat?
Are there ants at the pond?

They are there.
They're at the pond.
They're there.
At the pond.
There are ten men at the pond.
No! There's a bat at Sid's.
Pat's bat.
Ants are here, there, and everywhere.

WORD WORK 3.5 • WRITE

W W W W W W

W W W W W W

what _____

when_____

who _____

how _____

two _____

whose_____

10	11	12	13	14	15
15	14	13	12	11	10
11	10	12	11	15	13
14	T10	D15	P14	E11	I12
A13	B14	S12	M11	N15	O13
S14	M12	N13	O11	S15	N10

NUMBER WORK 3.2 • READ AND SAY

15	13	12	14	11	15
13	12	15	14	11	13
13	14	15	11	12	14
14S	11N	12M	S13	M15	N12

10:01

10:03

10:05

10:08

10:10

10:15

11:09

12:12

11:14

10:13

12:15

11:12

12:14

1:13

2:15

3:14

NUMBER WORK 3.4 • READ AND SAY

11:05	12:15	1:13	5:14	7:10	4:14
3:13	6:15	7:11	11:09	12:05	1:12
2:14	3:15	8:13	4:15	9:14	6:13

11 _____

12 _____

13 _____

14 _____

15 _____

NUMBER WORK 3.6 • LISTEN AND WRITE

_____ _____ _____ _____ _____ _____

_____ _____ _____ _____ _____ _____

_____ _____ _____ _____

_____ _____ _____ _____

:   :   :   :

_____ _____ _____ _____

:   :   :   :

_____ _____ _____ _____

11 = eleven   12 = twelve   13 = thirteen

14 = fourteen   15 = fifteen

NUMBER WORK 3.8 • READ

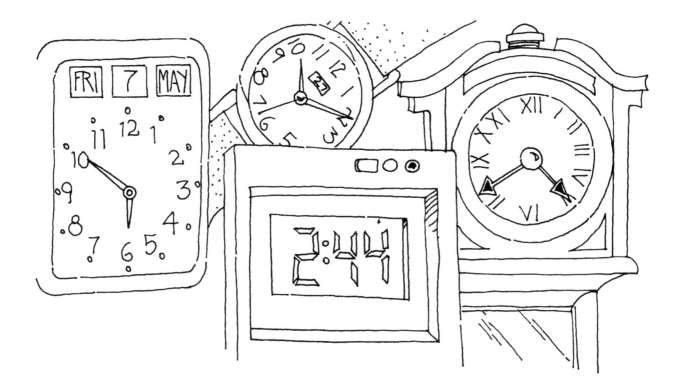

U L R BL PL SL BR DR PR

U u

pup	pub	putt	pud	pun
bub	but	bud	bus	bum	bun
tub	tut	dub	dud	dun
sup	sub	sud	sum	sun
mud	mutt	must	mum
nut	nun
Bud

bus	sun	tub	pub	pun	sub
nut	mum	Bud	bun	dud	bum
bud	sum	nun	putt	sup	spud
stud	stub	snub	stun	bust	dust

BUT:

one   son   done   does   doesn't   some   mother   brother   other

a mum   a pup   a spud   a bus   a tub

the sun   Sid's son   mud   nuts   subs

Is Bob at Four Brothers' Sub Stop?
No, but Bob's other brother Bud is at the Sub Stop.
Where's Bob? Is he at Dot's Spot?
No, but Tom is at Dot's Spot.

But where **is** Bob, at the pond?
He's on a bus.
What!

l

lap

lab

lad

lop

lob

lot

let

led

less

lip

lid

pill

L

Lamp

Lass

Land

Loss

List

Lest

Last

Lust

Lost

Lip

Lap

Lit   Let   Lot   List

bl	pl	sl
blab	plan	slap
blip	plot	slop
bled	plat	slam
blob	plus	slip
blot	plum	slum

SOUND-LETTER WORK 4.5 • READ AND SAY

lit	Bill	slap	led	sled	lest
lad	lip	bland	blend	lab	lands
Sal	blast	slob	lost	plan	pled
lots	plot	pill	till	less	mill
melt	mull	smell	sell	spell	spill
lamp	limp	blimp	letter	lesser	slipper
		seller	speller		

SOUND-LETTER WORK 4.6 • READ

Bill   Bill's pals   a sled   a lamp   a lab

pills   spam   land

L L L L

I I I

U U U

u u u u

bl _____

pl_____

sl_____

spell _____

sub_____

nut_____

Bill's pals sat on the sand with Bill. _____

_____

Bud is on a bus. _____

R r

rap	rem	rip
rat	rid	rad
rit	ram	rim
rot	rob	ran
Ron	rep	rub
ret	rut	red
rum	reb	run

br	**dr**	**pr**
brat	drat	pram
brass	dram	prim
Brad	drip	prep
bran	dress	press
Brit	drop	prop
brim	drub	prod
Brett	drum	prom

Brett	Brit	Ron	ran	dress	brass	rip	rap	rob
prep	drip	drop	prop	drum	rub	ram	rid	rest

Ron, Dan, Brad, and Brett run.
At the pond, Ron stops and rests. He sits.
Brett runs past Ron.
Dan runs past Ron.
Brad runs past Ron.
Then Dan runs past Brett and Brad.
At last, Ron stands and runs.
At the end, he's last.

Dan   Brett   Brad   Ron

R R R R

r r r r

Brenda pressed the dress. _____

_____

1 _____   2 _____   3 _____

4 _____   5 _____   6 _____

7 _____   8 _____   9 _____

10 _____   11 _____   12 _____

SOUND-LETTER WORK 4.13 • LISTEN AND SAY

A E I O M N
U u   L l   R r

p – u – p	n – u – t	t – u – b	s – t – u – n
l – a – b	l – e – t	s – l – i – p	s – p – e – l – l
r – u – n	r – e – d	d – r – i – p	p – r – e – s – s

 SOUND-LETTER WORK 4.14 • LISTEN AND WRITE

1 _____   2 _____   3 _____

4 _____   5 _____   6 _____

7 _____   8 _____   9 _____

SOUND-LETTER WORK 4.15 • SPELL (SAY)

bus   let   rip   lamp   rest   dust   lost   drum   land   drop

slap   dress   plan   spell   spill   slam   runs   letter   smell   brass

 WORD WORK 4.1 • LOOK, LISTEN, AND SAY

DO HAVE	**DON'T HAVEN'T**	**DOES HAS**	**DOESN'T HASN'T**
I have it.	Do you have it?	I do, but they don't.	
You have it.	Does he have it?	He does, but she doesn't.	
He has it.	Does she have it?	She does, but they don't.	
She has it.	Do we have it?	We do, but he doesn't.	
We have it.	Do they have it?	They do, but Bill doesn't.	
They have it.	Do you have it?	We do, but you don't.	
You have it.	Do I have it?	You do, but Bud doesn't.	

<table>
<tr><th>DID</th><th>HAD</th><th>DONE</th></tr>
</table>

DID	HAD	DONE
I had it.	Did you have it?	Yes I did, but they didn't.
I did it.	Have you done it?	No, I haven't.
She did it.	Has he done it?	No, he hasn't.
We did it.	Have they done it ?	No, they haven't.
Don did it.	Has Pam done it?	No, she hasn't.

WORD WORK 4.3 • READ

Bud: Bill, have you done it?

Bill: Done what?

Bud: It.

Bill: What's it?

Bud: That.

Bill: Oh, that! No, I haven't, but Britt has.

Bud: Britt has? Has Pam done it?

Bill: Pam hasn't done it.

WHAT IS IT? It's _____

NUMBER WORK 4.1 • LOOK, LISTEN, AND SAY

16	17	18	19	20
20	19	18	17	16
16	26	17	27	18
28	19	29	21	22
23	25	24	20	19
1910	1911	1912	1913	1914
1920	1817	1215	1716	1918

NUMBER WORK 4.2 • READ AND SAY

18	14	17	15	16
19	13	20	12	11
16	19	18	17	20
23	29	28	26	27
B17	P25	19A	U19	R24
16L	U2	L18	R16	U17

NUMBER WORK 4.3 • WRITE

16 _____

17 _____

18 _____

19 _____

20 _____

21 _____   22 _____   23 _____   24 _____   25 _____

NUMBER WORK 4.4 • LISTEN

PLUS

$1 + 1 = 2$ $1 + 1 = 2$
one and one is two   one plus one is two

Ten plus one is eleven.

NUMBER WORK 4.5 • WRITE AND SAY

10 + 1 = 11
Ten plus one is eleven.

10 + 11 = _____   8 + 7 = _____

8 + 8 = _____   10 + 7 = _____

11 + 8 = _____   12 + 6 = _____

19 + 8 = _____   11 + 18 = _____

15 + 11 = _____   15 + 13 = _____

NUMBER WORK 4.6 • LISTEN AND WRITE

_____   _____   _____   _____   _____

_____   _____   _____   _____   _____

_____   _____   _____   _____

_____   _____   _____   _____

_____   _____   _____   _____

_____   _____   _____   _____

-ED -ER TH

 ## SOUND-LETTER WORK 5.1 • LISTEN AND SAY

-ED

ed=/t/	ed=/d/	ed= /id/
tapped	tabbed	padded
dipped	stabbed	batted
tipped	sobbed	tested
stepped	dimmed	dusted
tossed	mobbed	landed
stopped	planned	lasted
missed	stunned	blotted
mopped	billed	rested

SOUND-LETTER WORK 5.2 • LOOK

tap + ed = tapped
trap + ed = trapped
tramp + ed = tramped
miss + ed = missed

SOUND-LETTER WORK 5.3 • READ AND SAY

tapped	tested	sobbed	planned	lasted
dusted	dimmed	landed	tabbed	batted
tipped	rested	missed	stepped	mopped

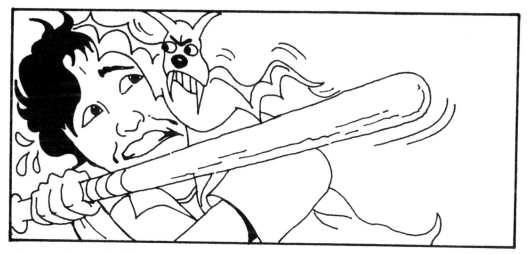

Deb stepped on Pat's bat. The bat was mad. It landed on Ed. Ed batted at the bat, but he missed. The bat stabbed Ed. Ed was stunned. Deb and Ed sobbed.

SOUND-LETTER WORK 5.5 • WRITE AN ANSWER

Did Ed do it? **Yes, he did it.**

Did Deb step on the bat? Yes, _____

Did the bat sob? Yes, _____

Did the bat and Ed sob? Yes, _____

Did Ed bat at the bat? Yes, _____

Who stopped at the pond? Brett stopped.

_____ Ed stepped on the bat.

_____ Brett rested.

_____ Bob planned the trip.

_____ Bill missed the bus.

_____ Pam passed the test.

SOUND-LETTER WORK 5.7 • LISTEN AND SAY

ER   er

better	batter	butter	pester
supper	dinner	matter	sender
inner	sitter	spinner	tester
madder	stopper	shipper	lender
sadder	letter	litter	speller

SOUND-LETTER WORK 5.8 • READ

Is Bill a better speller than Bob?   Yes, Bill's better.
Is Pam sadder than Dot?   No, Dot is sadder.
Is Sam madder than Dan.   No, Dan's madder.
Is Ben the sender of the letter.   Yes, Ben's the sender.

DO NOT LITTER!

Is this butter better? Yes, _____

Is that Ben's letter? Yes,_____

Is Ben the sender? Yes, _____

Does Bob have the letter? Yes, _____

Does it matter? Yes, _____

Is she the shipper? Yes, _____

Is Pat's brother a better speller? Yes, _____

_____

SOUND-LETTER WORK 5.10 • WRITE AN ANSWER

Is she the sender? No, _____

Does Ben have the letter? No, _____

Did you have dinner? No, _____

Is Dot sadder than Pam? No, _____

Did Bob have the letter? No, _____

Is Ed madder than the bat? No, _____

_____

SOUND-LETTER WORK 5.11 • LOOK, LISTEN, AND SAY

TH/th	TH/th
thin	the
thud	this
bath	that
moth	than
path	there
math	other
tenth	mother

SOUND-LETTER WORK 5.12A • READ AND SAY

The best path is there. That path is the other path. It's a bad path.

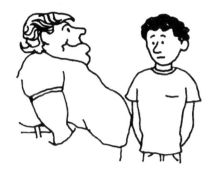

Bob is thin, but Bill is fat.

Beth does math in the bath.

This is a bat, and that is a moth.

It is the tenth.

SOUND-LETTER WORK 5.13 • WRITE

this _____

that _____

the _____

other _____

mother _____   brother _____   another_____   tenth _____

4th _____   5th _____   6th_____   7th _____

1 _____   2 _____   3 _____

4 _____   5 _____   6 _____

7 _____   8 _____   9 _____

10 _____   11 _____   12 _____

13 _____

O M N U L R H

s – t – e – p – p – e – d   m – i – s – s – e – d

p – l – a – n – n – e – d   r – e – s – t – e – d

b – e – t – t – e – r   b – u – t – t – e – r

m – o – t – h   m – o – t – h – e – r   t – h – a – t

1 _____   2 _____   3 _____

4 _____   5 _____   6 _____

7 _____   8 _____   9 _____

SOUND-LETTER WORK 5.17 • SPELL (SAY)

landed	stabbed	tossed	missed	tested
madder	letter	sitter	lender	spelled
this	bath	tenth	other	brother

WORD WORK 5.1 • LOOK, LISTEN, AND SAY

ON	OFF	FOR	OR
	OF	FROM	
	TO		

WORD WORK 5.2 • READ AND SAY

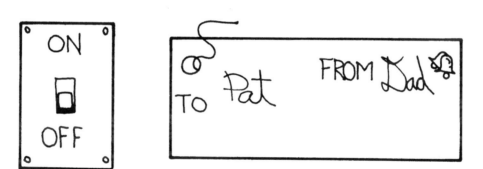

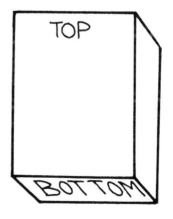

WORD WORK 5.3 • READ, ASK, AND ANSWER

Is the letter from Sid or for Sid? _____

_____

Is this to or from Tom? _____

_____

Is this the top of the bottom or the bottom of the top? _____

_____

Is that lamp on or off? _____

_____

WORD WORK 5.4 READ

What's this for?	It's for you.
For me?	Yes. It's from me.
	Look! From me to you.
But what's it for?	It's for this or that and here or there.
Hmm. Is this the top or the bottom?	That's the bottom of the top or the top of the bottom.
Is it on or off?	It's on off.
Is it off?	It's not on.
Then it's off.	Yes, it's on off.
Stop!	It is stopped; it's not on.
No! You stop!	

WORD WORK 5.5 • LISTEN, LOOK, AND SAY

1st	2nd	3rd	4th	5th
first	second	third	fourth	fifth

6th	7th	8th	9th	10th
sixth	seventh	eighth	ninth	tenth

WORD WORK 5.6 • READ

1st   4th   10th 2nd   5th   3rd   6th   9th 7th   8th

 WORD WORK 5.7 • LOOK, LISTEN, SAY

THIS MAN

THAT MAN

THESE MEN

THOSE MEN

NUMBER WORK 5.1 • LOOK, LISTEN, AND SAY

20	30	40	50
60	70	80	90
21	32	43	54
65	76	87	98
29	38	47	56
65	74	83	92

NUMBER WORK 5.2 • READ AND SAY

20	30	40	50
60	70	80	90
60	90	20	30
40	70	80	50
22	33	44	55
66	77	88	99

NUMBER WORK 5.3 • WRITE

30 _____   40 _____

50 _____   60 _____

70 _____   80 _____

90 _____

● .   . ●

thir ty   thir teen

30 pots   13 pots

40 spots   14 spots

50 moths   15 moths

60 letters   16 letters

70 pills   17 pills

80 nuts   18 nuts

90 men   19 men

NUMBER WORK 5.5 • LISTEN AND WRITE

_____   _____   _____   _____

_____   _____   _____   _____

_____   _____   _____   _____

_____   _____   _____   _____

REVIEW R1.1 • LOOK, LISTEN, AND SAY

Pat	Ted	Ed	Deb	Dad	Sid	Beth	Bob	Dot	Pam	Sam
Tim	Tom	Don	Ben	Dan	Bud	Sal	Bill	Ron	Brad	Brett

REVIEW R1.2 • READ AND SAY

Tim	Ted	Ron	Deb	Dan	Sid	Sal	Bob	Don	Pat	Brad
Pam	Tom	Ed	Ben	Dad	Bud	Beth	Bill	Dot	Brett	Sam

REVIEW R1.3 • READ

!

Stop the bus!   Pass the butter!

Snap the lid!   Press the pants!

Slap the pest!   Step on it!

Blast off!   Spell it!

DON'T STOP!   Don't do that!

Don't run!   Don't step on Pip!

Sam   Bud   Pam

I am Sam.   Who are you?
I am Bud.   Who is she?
She is Pam.   Who is he?

Ben   Brad   Brett

He is Ben.   Who are they?
They are Brad and Brett.
And who are we?
We are Sam and Bud.

Ted   Ed   Pat   Deb   Sid   Beth

Ted and Ed are brothers.
Pat and Deb are sisters.
Sid is Deb and Pat and Ed and Ted's dad.
Beth is Deb and Pat and Ed and Ted's mom.
Pip is Pat's pet bat.

Pip

REVIEW R1.6 • READ

Sam	Brad	Bill	Pam

What?	A 10-K run.
Where?	At Spot Pond.
When?	At ten.
Who?	Bill and Pam.
Where are Bill and Pam?	They're here at the pond.
Where are Bob and Ben.	They're there.
Where?	At Dot's Spot.

REVIEW R1.7 • READ

Ben, do you have a ten?   I don't have a ten, but I have ten ones.

Pam has a ten, doesn't she? She does. She has ten tens.

Who has ones? _____

REVIEW R1.8 • WRITE

Example: STOP > stop

DROP > _____   DRIP > _____   LOST > _____

DUST > _____   MEND > _____   MISS > _____

BLEND > _____   BUMP > _____   BEST > _____

LUMP > _____   RAMP > _____   BLAST > _____

STAND > _____   SNUB > _____   SPOT > _____

	A	E	I	O	U
P	pan				
B					
T			tin		
D					
S					sun

	A	E	I	O	U
S					
M					
N			in		
L					
R					

REVIEW R1.10 • LISTEN AND WRITE

1 _____   2 _____   3 _____

4 _____   5 _____   6 _____

7 _____   8 _____   9 _____

10 _____ 11 _____ 12 _____

C K G CK CL CR G GL GR

 SOUND-LETTER WORK 6.1 • LOOK, LISTEN, AND SAY

C   K

cat	kid	kiss	can	cap	Ken
cup	cop	kill	kip	cod	ken
Kit	cot	kin	Kent	cut	cud

SOUND-LETTER WORK 6.2 • LOOK

?ap = cap   ?ep = kep

?op = cop   ? ip = kip

?up = cup

 SOUND-LETTER WORK 6.3 • LOOK, LISTEN, AND SAY

ck	cl	cr
pack	clap	crack
pick	clip	crop
tick	clock	crib
buck	cluck	crest
deck	clad	crab
lock	club	crust

cab	cub	cad	cod	cud	cam	Ken	ked	kit	kiss
kill	back	tack	lack	rack	sack	lick	Rick	sick	Dick
peck	deck	tock	rock	sock	tuck	duck	suck	luck	crab
clock	crop	club	clam	clip	crib	crock	clip	clap	crust

cracker	packer	picker	ticker	locker	clipper

a backpack   a lock   a clock   a duck   a can   a tack

a rock   a sack   a deck   a cock   a kiss

Rick has bad luck. He lost his cap and backpack.

He locked his cat in the cab of his truck.

His truck is stuck in the muck.

His clock doesn't tick. He dropped it on a rock.

C C C

c c c

K K K K K

k k k k k

CL	click	___ock	___am	___op	___ap	___ip
CR	crab	___ock	___am	___op	___ib	___ack
CK	pack	sti___	ra___	ba___	stu___	ro___

SOUND-LETTER WORK 6.7 • LOOK, LISTEN, AND SAY

G   **g**

get   got   gap   God   Gus   gum   bag

bog   bug   beg   dog   pig   big

GL   **GR**

glob   glad   grad   grill

glass   glib   grid   grim

glum   gloss   grub   grab

SOUND-LETTER WORK 6.8 • READ AND SAY

gat   peg   gram   gut   big   grin   gun   sag   grab   gas
Meg   grass   mug   tag   grip   gull   grit   dig   nag   keg

SOUND-LETTER WORK 6.9 • READ

bug   bag   pig   dog   glass   grass

gun   gas   mug   tag   gull   Greg

SOUND-LETTER WORK 6.10 • READ

Gus got a dog. Meg was glad Gus got a dog, and not a pig.

Meg got a cat, but bugs got Gus's dog mad. The dog grabbed the cat. Then Meg got mad and grabbed the dog. Gus grabbed the cat. Meg got mad at Gus.

G G G G

g g g g

God		__us	__il
<u>g</u>et	__ot	__ap	__un
<u>g</u>lad	__ass	__ob	__um
<u>g</u>rass	__ad	__ab	__ub

. Bill glass a got <u>Bill got a glass.</u>

. grabbed Meg cat the _____

_____

. is grass the cat in The _____

_____

? Are the grass gulls the on _____

_____

? glad Meg not Is he did dog a get _____

_____

SOUND-LETTER WORK 6.12 • LISTEN AND WRITE

1 _____   2 _____   3 _____

4 _____   5 _____   6 _____

7 _____   8 _____   9 _____

10 _____

SOUND-LETTER WORK 6.13 • LISTEN AND SAY

C   **c**   **K**   **k**   **G**   **g**

ck   **cl**   **cr**   **gl**   **gr**

c – a – t   k – i – d   c – o – p   K – e – n

c – u – t   g – e – t   b – a – g   d – o – g

p – a – c – k   t – i – c – k   d – e – c – k   l – o – c – k

c – l – i – p   c – r – u – s – t   g – l – a – d   g – r – i – l – l

SOUND-LETTER WORK 6.14 • LISTEN AND WRITE

1 _____   2 _____   3 _____

4 _____   5 _____   6 _____

7 _____   8 _____   9 _____

SOUND-LETTER WORK 6.15 • LISTEN AND SAY

Ken: capital K – e – n   Dick: capital D – i – c – k

Gus: capital G – u – s   Greg: capital G – r – e – g

SOUND-LETTER WORK 6.16 • SPELL (SAY)

cab   Rick   luck   pick   Ken   gun   Meg   grass   Deb   Bill

clock   crack   Dick   Gus   Beth   gram   mug   deck   Greg

WORD WORK 6.1 • LOOK, LISTEN, AND SAY

NK	NG
sank	sang
sink	sing
tank	tang
stink	sting

WORD WORK 6.2 • READ AND SAY

drink   drank   drunk   sink   sank   sunk   sing   sang   sung

honk   long   hunk   hang   hung   bring   lung

blink   blank   spank   spunk   rink   ring

WORD WORK 6.3 • READ AND SAY

Batting, betting, ripping, blasting,
Dusting, ending, stepping, lasting,
Limping, blending, missing, planning,
Setting, sending, stopping, standing,
Testing, resting, nesting, fasting.

TH

thin	think	thing	thank
math	moth	path	bath	tenth

thud	thump	thunder	thug

thinker	sinker	tinker
thank	sank	tank
path	pat	pass
thin	tin	sin

WORD WORK 6.5 • READ AND SAY

Meg: I think Rick's truck is singing in the pond.

Greg: Singing? I think it's sinking.

Meg: I think his kids are sinking in the sand.

Greg: Sinking? I think they're singing.

NUMBER WORK 6.1 • LOOK, LISTEN, AND SAY

100	1,000	1,000,000	1,000,000,000
101	105	120	250	370
1,100	1,101	1,230	1,740	1,860
3,090	5,280	3,200,000	5,900,000

NUMBER WORK 6.2 • READ AND SAY

100	300	500	700	900
2,000	4,000	6,000	8,000	10,000
650	470	390	560	780
220	830	940	125	365
1,239	2,758	4,631	9,999	10,560
3,000,000	5,500,000	7,850,000	9,275,000,000

NUMBER WORK 6.3 • LISTEN, WRITE, AND SAY

A _____ B _____ C _____ D _____

E _____ F _____ G _____ H _____

I _____ J _____ K _____ L _____

M _____ N _____ O _____ P _____

Q _____ R _____ S _____ T _____

U _____ V _____ W _____ X _____

Y _____ Z _____

H SH CH TCH A..E AY AI

 ## SOUND-LETTER WORK 7.1 • LOOK, LISTEN, AND SAY

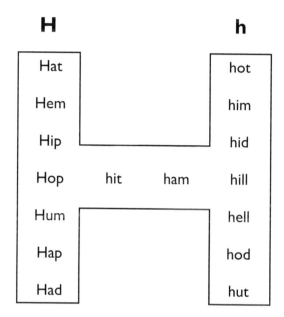

SOUND-LETTER WORK 7.2 • READ AND SAY

hit	ham	hop	hang	hub	hem
hill	hack	has	hog	him	his
hut	hum	hen	hell	hunk	Hank

SH	**CH**	**TCH**
shack	chat	patch
shed	check	pitch
dish	rich	retch
rash	chop	ditch
shun	such	latch

SOUND-LETTER WORK 7.4 • READ AND SAY

shot	chop	rush	catch	batch	dash
stitch	mush	much	rich	shop	chick
match	Chuck	shock	ship	shut	shell
chest	batch	bash	crutch	shall	pitch

SOUND-LETTER WORK 7.5 • READ

Chuck and Hal had lunch with chopsticks on a ship.

Hal had ham, but Chuck had hash for lunch.

At dinner, Hal had hash, and Chuck had chops.

At supper they had chicken.

SOUND-LETTER WORK 7.6 • WRITE

SH shack   ____ut   ____ock   di____   da____   ru____

CH chill   ____ip   ____eck   mu____   su____   ri____

TCH catch   ha____   sti____   ma____   la____   Mi____

SOUND-LETTER WORK 7.7 • LISTEN AND WRITE

I _____   2 _____   3 _____

4 _____   5 _____   6 _____

7 _____   8 _____   9 _____

10 _____

_____

SOUND-LETTER WORK 7.8 • LOOK, LISTEN, AND SAY

AY	AI	A . . E	
pay	paid	ape	share
bay	main	ate	stare
day	rain	paste	case
may	stain	date	dare
lay	lain	sale	came

AND: great, break, steak

SOUND-LETTER WORK 7.9 • READ AND SAY

say	make	base	bake	aim	tape	Ray	taste	laid	mail	date
take	gay	nail	cake	hair	hay	name	late	gray	play	rate
made	air	same	base	spare	chair	Dane	male	sail	stray	cape

SOUND-LETTER WORK 7.10 • READ

Ray may stay in Spain, but there is rain in Spain. The rain in Spain is in the plains, so Ray may sail at the cape. In May the days are fair there.

Dale baked a cake. It tasted great. She shared the cake with May. When May ate the cake she said, "This cake is great. Did you make it?" Later that day, May shared the cake with Ray.

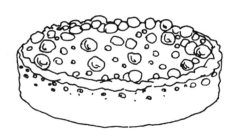

SOUND-LETTER WORK 7.11A • WRITE

ma____   sta____   Ra____   pl____   the____

da____   gra____   Who baked the cake?_____

Who ate the cake? _____ and _____

SOUND-LETTER WORK 7.12 • WRITE A QUESTION

Where **did he stay?** He stayed **in Spain.**

Where _____ He may sail **at the cape.**

What _____ She baked **a cake.**

Who _____ **May** ate the cake.

How _____ It tasted **great.**

When _____ The days are fair **in May.**

SOUND-LETTER WORK 7.13 • LISTEN AND WRITE

1 _____   2_____   3_____

4 _____   5_____   6_____

7 _____   8_____   9_____

10 _____

SOUND-LETTER WORK 7.14 • LISTEN AND SAY

H   h   sh   ch   tch   y   ay   ai

s – a – y   h – e – m   h – i – m   d – i – s – h   c – h – a – t

c – a – t – c – h   p – a – y   r – a – i – n   a – t – e   s – t – a – y

 SOUND-LETTER WORK 7.15 • LISTEN AND WRITE

I _____   2_____   3 _____

4 _____   5_____   6 _____

SOUND-LETTER WORK 7.16 • SPELL (SAY)

Hal   Chuck   Ray   Dale   May   Spain   Dane

hang   check   pitch   plains   shock   match

 WORD WORK 7.1 • LOOK, LISTEN, AND SAY

I   (to) me   we   (to) us

            you   (to) you

he   (to) him

she   (to) her   they   (to) them

it   (to) it

WORD WORK 7.2 • READ AND SAY

She hit me.

Meg, did you hit him?

Yes, but he hit me.

Did you hit her?

Yes, but she and Kit hit me.

Meg, did you and Kit hit him?

Yes, but he and Dick hit us.

Dick, did you and Tim hit them?

Yes, we did.

WORD WORK 7.3 • WRITE AN ANSWER

Who hit Meg? _____

Who hit Tim? _____

Who hit Meg and Kit? _____

Meg, who hit you? _____

Meg and Kit, who hit you? _____

WORD WORK 7.4 • LOOK, LISTEN, AND SAY

I	me	my	we	us	our
you	you	your	you	you	your
he	him	his	they	them	their
she	her	her			
it	it	its			
who	whom	whose			

Pat: Where is your hat?

Matt: It's in my pack.

Pat: Whose hat is this?

Matt: I think it's his hat.

Pat: Whose hat?

Matt: Bob's.

Pat: And whose hat is that?

Matt: That's her hat.

Pat: Whose? Pam's?

Matt: No. Deb's.

Pat: Matt, where are our packs?

Matt: Our packs are there.

Pat: Then whose packs are these?

Matt: These are their packs.

Pat: Whose, Matt, whose?

Matt: Chuck and Hal's.

Pat: Where's Meg's pack? It isn't here.

Matt: It doesn't have straps.

Pat: Why not?

Matt: Meg got mad and cut off its straps.

Pat: When Meg is mad, she's bad.

Where is my pen?   **Your pen is here.**
_____

Where is your pen? _____

Where is Dan's pen? _____

Where are Bud and Bill's packs ? _____

Where are your and my hats? _____

Where is May's dress? _____

Where is my dog? _____

Where is the dog's dish? _____

MAY

Sunday	Monday	Tuesday	Wednesday	Thursday	Friday	Saturday
	1	2	3	4	5	6
7	8	9	10	11	12	13
14	15	16	17	18	19	20
21	22	23	24	25	26	27
28	29	30	31			

first (1st)   second (2nd)   third (3rd)   fourth (4th)   fifth (5th)

sixth (6th)   seventh (7th)   eighth (8th)   ninth (9th)   tenth (10th)

twentieth (20th)   thirtieth (30th)

WORD WORK 7.8 • ANSWER

What day is today?   (3) <u>**It's Wednesday, the third.**</u>

(7) _____

(5) _____

(6) _____

(1) _____

(4) _____

(2) _____

UNIT 8   E EE EA Y I..E IE IGH

SOUND-LETTER WORK 8.1 • LOOK, LISTEN, AND SAY

E	EE	E..E	EA	EA..E	Y
be	see	here	eat	ease	Betty
me	seem	Pete	meat	please	baby
he	need	theme	real	tease	chilly
she	sleep	these	steal	crease	hairy

SOUND-LETTER WORK 8.2 • READ AND SAY

we   seat   buggy   he   seen   neat   Pete   sheep   heat   heal

she   bleed   tee   ease   beet   deal   sandy   hilly   be   sloppy

muddy   east   dream   here   sheet   seek   meal   bee

Greek   lead   mossy   rainy   easy   glassy   theme

cheap   dusty   east   steer   me   Kathy   keep   Easter

Betty   seem   these   please

SOUND-LETTER WORK 8.3A • READ

Pete thinks it's neat to be seen
speaking Greek. Between you and
me, it's no big deal, but he needs
to feel like a big cheese.

We have a cabin in a hilly place at Great East Lake. The hills are steep, and the lake is deep. There's a sandy beach near a clear stream. The air is crisp and clean. We don't feel the heat in summer. It's even chilly in the evening. It's a great place to rest and sleep. It's neat.

SOUND-LETTERWORK 8.4 • WRITE

a lot of hills **Yes, it's really hilly.**

a lot of bugs **Yes, it's really** _____

a lot of mud _____

a lot of rain _____

a lot of dust _____

a lot of sand _____

a big mess _____

SOUND-LETTER WORK 8.5 • LISTEN AND WRITE

1 _____   2 _____   3 _____

4 _____   5 _____   6 _____

7 _____   8 _____   9 _____

10 _____

SOUND-LETTER WORK 8.6 • LOOK, LISTEN, AND SAY

I..E	Y	IGH	IE
pipe	by	high	pie
bite	sty	sigh	tie
time	my	might	die
dime	shy	night	lie
side	cry	right	

SOUND-LETTER WORK 8.7 • READ AND SAY

pile	type	sight	pine	hype	light	tide	dry	tile	slight
tired	dine	lite	try	lime	pry	mine	sly	mile	ply
nine	glide	hide	hire	ripe	site	pride	bride	slide	sigh

SOUND-LETTER WORK 8.8 • LOOK AND LISTEN

four   five   father   fee   free   flee   fly

Mike and I had a nice time on the Nile for three days and two nights. We biked beside the Nile for nineteen miles. Then we hiked another nine miles into the hills to see King Tut's Mine. We came to a sign that said "fly in the sky at Ace's Place."

SOUND-LETTER WORK 8.10 • READ

"Let's fly in the sky," said Mike.

"Why?" said I.

"Why not?" he said.

"OK, that's fine," I lied.

But I tried.

So we decided to fly.

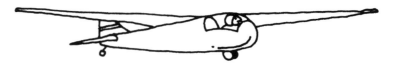

We had a nice ride, side by side inside Ace's glider, high in the sky. But as for flying,

I'd rather fly kites.

pine tree <u>You can see a lot of pine trees at the lake.</u>

time _____

dime _____

side _____

nine _____

cry _____

high _____

might _____

light _____

tired _____

SOUND-LETTER WORK 8.12 • LISTEN AND WRITE

1 _____   2 _____   3 _____

4 _____   5 _____   6 _____

7 _____   8 _____   9 _____

10 _____

E	EE	EA	Y	IGH	IE

s – h – e   s – l – e – e – p   s – t – e – a – l

p – l – e – a – s – e   c – h – i – l – l – y   t – i – m – e

c – r – y   n – i – g – h - t   p – i – e

 SOUND-LETTER WORK 8.14 • LISTEN AND WRITE

1 _____   2_____   3_____

4 _____   5_____   6_____

SOUND-LETTER WORK 8.15 • SPELL (SAY)

seat	sheep	meal	dimes
muddy	rainy	right	side
Greek	Kathy	Betty	Mike

 WORD WORK 8.1 • LISTEN AND SAY

Whose? Mine.

I	me	my	mine		we	us	our	ours
you	you	your	yours		you	you	your	yours
he	him	his	his		they	them	their	theirs
she	her	her	hers					

This is my seat. It's *mine*.

This is your seat. It's *yours*.

This is his seat. It's *his*.

This is her seat. It's *hers*.

These are our seats. They're *ours*.

These are their seats. They're *theirs*.

This is mine. Is this *yours*?

This is his. Is this *hers*?

This is ours. Is this *theirs*?

WORD WORK 8.3 • READ

Listen up, kids. We need to clean this place up.

Whose pack is that?

It's mine.

OK, Teddy, pick it up.

Whose pants are these?

They're his.

OK, Chuck, pick them up.

Whose hat is this?

It's hers.

OK, Pam, pick it up.

Whose bags are these?

They're ours.

OK, Bobby and Billy, pick them up.

Whose caps are these?

They're theirs.

OK, Dale and Ray, pick them up.

Pam, is this hat yours? **Yes, it's mine.**

Bill, is this hat Pam's? _____

Chuck, is this pack Ted's? _____

Bob and Bill, are these bags yours? _____

Ted, are these caps Dale and Ray's? _____

Chuck, are these pants yours? _____

Is this chair mine? _____

Are these seats ours? _____

WORD WORK 8.5 • LISTEN AND SAY

—'LL

I'll	you'll	he'll	she'll	it'll	we'll	they'll

Ted'll	Meg'll	Pat'll	Deb'll	Bob'll

—LE

able	table	cable	maple	staple	idle	cycle	people

bubble	hobble	babble	saddle	double	trouble

WORD WORK 8.6 • READ

We'll get cable TV. We'll be able to place it on the maple table.

She'll get some double bubble gum and a bottle of pop.

I'll bet those people are in trouble.

They'll place the saddle on the hobbled horse.

 ## WORD WORK 8.7 • LISTEN AND SAY

• .	. •
glider	defy
flying	review
listen	beside
summer	between
cabin	agree
dinner	assist
accent	attend
acid	delay

 ## WORD WORK 8.8 • LISTEN AND SAY

Chile	Benin	China	Gabon	Congo	Iran	Ghana	Japan
Iceland	Nepal	Mali	Peru	Russia	Sudan	Tonga	Ukraine

FLYING
IN CHINA
by
A.M. Ming

GLIDING
IN PERU
by
Carlos C.
Castro

DELAYED
IN GHANA
by
I.M. Nkoma

DINNER
IN JAPAN
by
Betty D. Smith

SUMMER
IN CHILE
by
E.H. Hopkins

A CABIN
IN
ICELAND
by
R.C. Konrad

A RUSSIAN
ACCENT
by
K.G. Lipski

KITES
IN IRAN
by
I.E. Agha

SUDAN
DEFIED
by
L.P. Mungari

INSIDE
NEPAL
by
S.T. Thomas

BETWEEN
CONGO
AND
GABON
by
R.U. Stanley

THE BENIN
REVIEW
by
R. Mama

Aa   *Bb*   *Cc*   *Dd*   *Ee*

Ace   Bea   Cece   Deb   Ed

Ace   *Bea*   *Cece* *Deb*   *Ed*

HANDWRITING 8.2 • READ

ace   *add*   *bad*   *cede* *dab*

ebb   *cab*   *dead* *bed*   *cad*

Ace   *Bea*   *Cece* *Deb*   *Ed*

C /K/

cab   cob   cub

C /S/

cell   city   cent   citrus   center   cinema

AND:

ace   dice   pace   mice   race

nice   place   lice   trace   nice

BUT:

since   Vince   France   dance   piece   peace

lice   mace   cell   price   cat   lace   rice   place   cub   slice   trace

spice   cellar   center   cop   cinema   citrus   can   space   cents   city

Cindy is in the city.
I think she's at Circle Park,
but Candy is in another place.
I think she's at Center Cinema
or maybe she's at the circus.

The price on this rice can't be right.

Ace ran a ten-mile race.
He set the pace.
He got second place.

 SOUND-LETTER WORK 9.4 • LOOK, LISTEN, AND SAY

CEI	**EI**
ceiling	either
receive	neither
receipt	
deceive	
conceive	

 SOUND-LETTER WORK 9.5 • LISTEN AND WRITE

1 _____ 2 _____ 3 _____

4 _____ 5 _____ 6 _____

7 _____ 8 _____ 9 _____

10 _____

SOUND-LETTER WORK 9.6 • LOOK, LISTEN, AND SAY

F

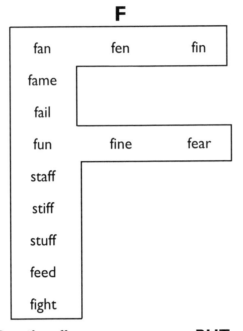

fan	fen	fin
fame		
fail		
fun	fine	fear
staff		
stiff		
stuff		
feed		
fight		

AND: if off   **BUT:** of

SOUND-LETTER WORK 9.7 • READ

fat	fast	fad	fact	fate	fame	fell	left	fed
fit	fib	fun	drift	lift	safe	feel	leaf	life
reef	thief	fight	feeble	fish	fight	fuss	funny	fair
fine	left	fan	face	off	after	offer	iffy	fob

 SOUND-LETTER WORK 9.8 • LISTEN AND SAY

FL	**FR**
flat	frat
flee	free
fly	fry
flog	frog
flight	fright

96 ● FROM SOUND TO SENTENCE

SOUND-LETTER WORK 9.9 • READ

flash	flesh	fresh	flit	frill	flop	frost	flub	frame
flame	flea	freak	flog	fried	flip	Fran	floppy	frosty
fly	Fred	fled	flight	Frank	flog	flay	flipper	free

SOUND-LETTER WORK 9.10A • LOOK, LISTEN, AND SAY

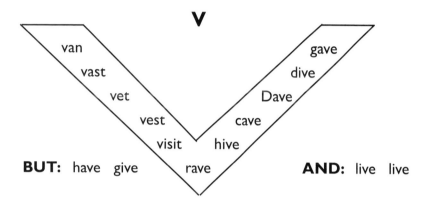

V

van
vast
vet
vest
visit
gave
dive
Dave
cave
hive

BUT: have give rave **AND:** live live

SOUND-LETTER WORK 9.10B • READ AND SAY

save	vet	rave	give	cave	van	vim	live	drive
vast	shave	vat	vest	have	leave	visit	river	Dave

SOUND-LETTER WORK 9.11 • READ

Flash is very fat. He has a van. He drives very fast in his van. In fact, fat Flash drives too fast. Flash is not a safe driver. A cop stopped Flash. Flash paid a fine. Flash's face is red.

Vinnie lives in a cave. He never shaves.
At night he fries frogs legs and raves.

Fred is very frank. He speaks his mind freely. If he doesn't like something, he will say so. His brother Frank is not frank. He never speaks his mind. He finds it difficult to speak freely.

The other night at supper Fred said to his mother, "I hate your fried chicken." His mother's face became flaming red. She flipped out. She gave Fred's fried chicken to Frank.

Frank likes fried chicken. He can eat four legs, five thighs, and at least three breasts. He ate a lot of chicken. At night Fred was hungry and he went to the refrigerator for a snack. It was full of chicken.

SOUND-LETTER WORK 9.12 • WRITE

F F F F F

f f f f

V V V V V

v v v v v

four _____

fourteen _____

forty _____

five _____   fifteen _____   fifty _____

seven _____   seventeen _____   seventy _____

50 <u>fifty</u> _____   4 _____   17 _____   5 _____

14 _____   44 _____   55 _____

74 _____   75 _____

1775 _____

SOUND-LETTER WORK 9.13 • LISTEN AND SAY

O

mother	brother	son	other	another	some
one	done	somebody	someone	hover	love
lover	glove	above	honey	money	

SOUND-LETTER WORK 9.14 • READ

Three little kittens lost their mittens, and the kittens' one brother lost his gloves. The kittens' and brother's mother loves her daughters and son, but she will not get another pair of mittens or gloves for her kids. She has some money, but she doesn't have much honey, and she needs some money to get the honey.

SOUND-LETTER WORK 9.15 • LISTEN AND WRITE

1 _____ 2 _____ 3 _____

4 _____ 5 _____ 6 _____

7 _____ 8 _____ 9 _____

10 _____

_____

SOUND-LETTER WORK 9.16 • LISTEN AND SAY

C c   **F f**   **V v**   **FL fl**   **FR fr**

c – i – t – y   c – e – n – t   c – e – i – l – i – n – g

f – u – n   s – t – u – f – f   f – i – g – h – t

g – a – v – e   v – a – n   l – e – a – v – e

SOUND-LETTER WORK 9.17 • LISTEN AND WRITE

1 _____ 2 _____ 3 _____

4 _____ 5 _____ 6 _____

7 _____ 8 _____ 9 _____

SOUND-LETTER WORK 9.18 • SPELL (SAY)

center   price   offer   vest

nice   river   fail   have

place   vest   drive   safe

WORD WORK 9.1 • LISTEN AND SAY

EY

key   money   honey   monkey

WORD WORK 9.2 • READ

Have you got the keys and the money, honey?
I've got the keys, but not the money.
That's funny. Where is the money?
Your pet monkey ate the money.

 WORD WORK 9.3 • LISTEN AND SAY

● ᐧ ᐧ	ᐧ ● ᐧ
syllable	accepted
consonant	delighted
motorist	remember
bicycle	another
accident	September
cinema	October
minimum	November
hospital	December
ambulance	receiver

There was an accident near the cinema. A motorist hit a bicyclist. An ambulance came from the hospital. It hit an animal. The motorist was OK, the animal was simply stunned and ran off, but the bicyclist went to the hospital in the ambulance.

Another September has come. I remember last September. We were in New Brunswick. It was delightful. October was beautiful, but the weather in November was terrible—cold and rainy. In December we went back to dry and sunny Nevada.

WORD WORK 9.6 • LISTEN AND SAY

EA

head   dead   lead   read   instead   tread   weather

BUT: great   steak   break

BUT: breakfast

WORD WORK 9.7 • READ AND SAY

Have you read the paper today?

No, I didn't. What did it say?

There was an accident at the lead mine. The headline said "ten dead."

Really? That's dreadful.

WORD WORK 9.8 • READ

Brett took a morning break and had a great breakfast at Dot's Place. Instead of bread and honey with cheese and apple pie, he ate steak and eggs. After he ate, he read the headlines in the Leadville Sentinel.

When he came back from his break, his boss Brent said, "You're late coming back from your break. Where is your head? So if you want to earn bread, get the lead out of your pants and break a leg."

 WORD WORK 9.9 • LISTEN AND SAY

TI

● •	• ● •	• • ● •
action	collection	satisfaction
section	correction	recreation
fiction	attention	destination
suction	reflection	constitution
friction	attraction	comprehension
traction	emotion	celebration

REVOLUTION

TRANSAVANNA CITY 10/26 (IP) There was a revolution yesterday in Transavanna. There was fighting in the streets. There was a lot of action near Celebration Park. Supporters of the Constitution Party confronted members of the Reaction Faction. One section of the city was in flames. The army refused to defend the Presidential Palace. The president is being held in detention. The leaders of the Constitution Party are demanding democratic elections.

HANDWRITING WORK 9.1 • LOOK

Ff	*Gg*	*Rr*
Fred	Grace	Reggie
Fred	*Grace*	*Reggie*
age	*free*	*race*

HANDWRITING WORK 9.2 • READ

face	*gear*	*reef*	*cafe*
egg	*bear*	*barge*	*grab*
Greg	*Reggie*	*Brad*	*Fred*

REVIEW R2.1 • READ AND SAY

Hal	Cal	Candy	Kathy	Meg	Greg	Betty	Dick	Rick	Van
Kit	Cindy	Chuck	Gus	Ray	May	Dale	Pete	Fred	Fran

REVIEW R2.2 • READ

"I'm glad you came," said Greg to Meg, "but the clock says ten, and we're late. The others have left for the lake."

"Do you think we can catch them?" asked Meg.

"We'll take the path by the creek. It leads to the lake."

"But Greg, did you bring our lunch and the drinks and the ice?"

"I did, so let's race up the creek to the lake."

"I'll beat you," said Meg. So they raced to the lake with the lunch.

"We're near," said Meg. "Hush, I hear singing."

Greg stopped to listen, but Meg raced on and beat Greg to the lake.

So they dined on sandwiches, chicken, and rice, and a slice of lemon pie. Then they sailed on the lake.

"What a high," said Meg with a sigh.

At five o'clock, the fun wasn't finished.

"Let's dance," cried Fran, and they danced till eleven that night.

At breakfast, Fran's mother asked, "Was it nice?"

"It was great," grinned Fran, "a fine time."

REVIEW R2.3 • WRITE

I see it.		to __e	_y pen	It's __e
You see it.	to _____	_____ pen	It's _____ .
He sees it.	_____	_____	_____
She sees it.	_____	_____	_____
It sees me.	_____	_____	_____
We see it.	_____	_____	_____
They see it.	_____	_____	_____

REVIEW R2.4 • READ

In September Frank spent a lot of money at Center City Cinema. In fact, he spent his last cent on candy. He loves action films. He thinks his favorites are *The Living Dead* and *Impossible Flight*. Frank even took his pet frog to see *Frogmen in Action*. Frank is Fred Cisco's biggest fan, and he also likes Frances Spicer, his favorite actress.

Frank made a list of his favorite films. Here they are:

The Big Fight — *it's great.*
Ice in December — *a fine film*
Dead of the Night — *scary*
I Fly Fighters — *full of action*
The Price of Money — *clever story*
Seven Brothers in Love — *fun and funny*
Kathy's Last Dance — *sweet but sad*
Revolution — *thrilling*
The French Thief — *a great cops-and-robbers flick*
Breaking Up — *a nice Frances Spicer film*

c <u>cent</u>   k _____   C _____

K _____   ck _____   cl _____

cr _____   _____   g _____

gl _____   gr _____   nk _____   _____

ng _____   th _____   _____   h _____

H _____   sh _____   _____   ch _____

ch _____   Ch _____   tch _____   _____

a..e _____   _____   ay _____   _____

ai _____   _____   e _____   _____

ee _____   _____   ea _____   _____

y _____   _____   ey _____   ei _____

i..e _____   _____   ie _____   _____

igh _____   _____   f _____   v _____

F _____   V _____   Gr _____   Fr _____

fl _____   fr _____   'll _____   ble _____

O OW O..E OA OR AU A AW AR OU O

SOUND-LETTER WORK 10.1 • LOOK, LISTEN, AND SAY

O	OW	O..E	OA	OR	OR ..E
no	bow	robe	coat	born	tore
go	tow	pope	soap	fork	shore
so	low	rope	load	corn	before
old	mow	tote	goad	port	store

AND: The court is on the fourth floor. There's a sign on the door.

SOUND-LETTER WORK 10.2 • READ

told	row	note	sold	show	vote	hold	grow	rode	road
fold	blow	code	toad	gold	slow	rose	close	boat	roll
pose	toll	or	for	only	open	short	fort	cord	torn

BUT: do   does   to   two

SOUND-LETTER WORK 10.3 • READ

Let me show you Rosie Golden's home. She was born here in forty-four and lived here until seventy-four. That was before she went to New York and acted in Broadway shows and, later, soap operas. But every summer she came back to her old home here at the shore.

She loved to grow roses and row her little boat around the cove. Often in the evening she rowed her boat out of the port and along the coast, throwing roses overboard to see them float.

One morning when Rosie was over eighty years old, they found her boat on the shore. In it was a note. It only said, "Rose is no more, but the roses are yours."

SOUND-LETTER WORK 10.4 • WRITE

SLOW _____   Will _____   Wade _____

grow _____   flow _____   blow _____

Rose _____   fourth _____   morning _____

SOUND-LETTER WORK 10.5 • WRITE IT RIGHT

Let's / to the shore. / row _____

Rose / the boat. / rowed _____

The store / open. / was not _____

It / closed today. / is _____

SOUND-LETTER WORK 10.6 • LISTEN AND WRITE

1 _____   2 _____   3 _____

4 _____   5 _____   6 _____

7 _____   8 _____   9 _____

10 _____

SOUND-LETTER WORK 10.7 • LOOK, LISTEN, AND SAY

AU	A	AW	AR	OU	O
Paul	all	saw	war	ought	long
haul	tall	law	warn	thought	lost
caught	call	raw	ward	bought	cost
taught	fall	paw	wart	fought	log

SOUND-LETTER WORK 10.8 • READ AND SAY

draw   flaw   claw   thaw   straw   warp   wall   lawyer   prawn

fraud   sought   taunt   haunted

Walk your talk.   Wash it with water.   The ball is lost.

Call me at the mall.   Let's draw straws.   Paul caught the ball.

BUT: aunt

SOUND-LETTER WORK 10.9 • READ

Saul: Do you remember Paul Walker? He's in Washington.

Wally: Really? I always thought he would be a great lawyer. He studied law at Rawson College, didn't he? Is he practicing law in Washington?

Saul: Well, he called yesterday. He wanted advice. We talked and talked. After he finished at Rawson State he played baseball for the Great Falls Hawks.

Wally: Yeah, he was an all-star player in college.

Saul: He was going to start practicing law in the fall with Hawkins, Long, and Walker, his dad's law office.

Wally: But he's in Washington.

Saul: Yeah. He got a call from the Washington Nationals baseball team. They offered a contract—a lot of money. So he decided to play ball.

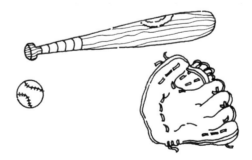

yesterday..bought. **Yesterday I bought a ball.**

talked .. Paul _____

walked .. mall _____

called .. U-Haul _____

thought .. lawyer _____

taught .. college _____

washed .. wall _____

SOUND-LETTER WORK 10.11 • LISTEN AND WRITE

1 _____   2 _____   3 _____

4 _____   5 _____   6 _____

7 _____   8 _____   9 _____

10 _____

SOUND-LETTER WORK 10.12 • LISTEN AND SAY

W w

s – l – o – w   w – a – i – t   w – h – y

w – a – s – h – e – d   l – a – w – y – e – r   s – t – r – a – w

low	fall	store	Rose
coat	raw	throw	taught
row	born	Paul	warm
slow	thought	Saul	wall

SOUND-LETTER WORK 10.14 • LISTEN AND WRITE

1 _____   2 _____   3 _____

4 _____   5 _____   6 _____

7 _____   8 _____   9 _____

WORD WORK 10.1 • LISTEN AND SAY

KN	H	B
know	hour	comb
knock	honest	lamb
knot	honor	dumb
knife		bomb
knee		limb
		climb
		debt

A knock at the door!

At this hour? At one in the morning? Who's there?

I don't know.

I can't untie this knot in the rope.

Then cut it with a knife.

Ay yay yay! I cut my knee.

Honesty is always our policy

WE HONOR ALL CREDIT CARDS

USE: *knife, honest, honor, knot, knock, hour, know, honorable*

_____ on wood   an _____ ago

tied up in _____ s   an _____ student

I don't _____   _____ , fork, and spoon

an_____ man   on my _____

WORD WORK 10.4 • LOOK, LISTEN, AND SAY

W

wet	win	wait	wide	we
web	will	way	wipe	week
west	wind	waste	wife	weak
well	wish	wake	wine	weed

AND: wear, weather

WORD WORK 10.5. • READ AND SAY

wed	wage	wave	waist	wake	witch
winter	waiter	windy	weekly	weak	

 WORD WORK 10.6 • LOOK, LISTEN, AND SAY

Y

yes	yet	yell	yam	year
		yesterday		

WORD WORK 10.7 • READ AND SAY

you	yellow	yield	yoga	Yukon

Yesterday Will went west with Ed. They wanted to see the wide open spaces of the West. First they went to Yellowstone. They were there one week. The weather was wet and windy. Then they went to the Yukon. The weather there wasn't much better. They wished they had

  waited for the weather to be better. They wasted two weeks. Yet, they were happy they went. "Well," said Will to his wife, when they went home, "We'll go again in a year."

WORD WORK 10.9 • WRITE WITH "W" OR "Y"

___ent	___est	___ou	___esterda___	___ild
___ield	onl___	the___	___e'll	___ind
___et	___et	___ell	___ell	___ear	___ear

HANDWRITING WORK 10.1 • LOOK

Hal has   Ida is   Lisa lets   Sid says

Hal has   Ida is   Lisa lets   Sid says

HANDWRITING WORK 10.2 • READ

head high chill ice idea
lead sell sigh has case
Halil Isabella Liberia Seba

UNIT 11   # J G DG U OO UE U..E EW

SOUND-LETTER WORK 11.1 • LOOK, LISTEN, AND SAY

J	G	DG
jam	gem	edge
jet	gin	badge
just	gist	fudge
joke	age	ridge

SOUND-LETTER WORK 11.2 • READ AND SAY

Jim	Joe	Jan	Jack	Jill	Jed	George	June	July
Japan	Germany	jock	nudge	jog	stage	jive	rage	judge
cage	just	wages	jump	fridge	garage	Grace	joke	

SOUND-LETTER WORK 11.3 • READ

Jonathan needed a new auto. His old jalopy was dead. It was a piece of junk. So he drove it to Joe's Junk Yard and sold it for just fifty dollars. Then he went to Jim's GM Garage. He looked at a GM Giant, but it was very big. He tried the Ranger. It was nice, but the engine was big, and the gas mileage was bad — only twelve miles per gallon. The salesman told Jonathan, "This Ranger is a gem. And no payments till July. Grab it before it's gone." But Jonathan decided to shop some more.

At Jerry's Foreign Auto he looked at a German model and a Japanese car. The German car, a Jetstream, was gorgeous, but beyond Jonathan's budget. His wages weren't enough to buy a new car. He tried the Fuji Ninja. It was one year old, small, and cheaper. The salesman told him, "Jump in and drive it to the junction and over the Jellystone Bridge." He did, and he liked it, but there was just one problem; it was bright orange.

FROM SOUND TO SENTENCE ● **117**

J J J

j j j

Jack _____   Jill _____   Joe _____

jar _____   judge _____   jet _____

SOUND-LETTER WORK 11.5 • WRITE A SENTENCE WITH THESE WORDS

a jar of jam _____

good gas mileage _____

a great engine _____

an orange jump suit _____

judge and jury _____

SOUND-LETTER WORK 11.6 • LISTEN AND WRITE

1 _____   2 _____   3 _____

4 _____   5 _____   6 _____

7 _____   8 _____   9 _____

10 _____

_____

 SOUND-LETTER WORK 11.7 • LOOK, LISTEN, AND SAY

U	OO
put	book
pull	good
push	look
bull	cook

AND: would   could   should

SOUND-LETTER WORK 11.8 • READ

took	wood	full	foot	shook	crook	wool
hook	hood	stood	pudding	push	pull	should

SOUND-LETTER WORK 11.9 • READ

He took just one look at the cook book and then cooked a good meal. And for dessert he made a pudding that was so good I ate too much, and now I'm really full. I think he should have been a cook. He could have opened a restaurant and made a lot of money. Then he would have become rich, and he wouldn't have become a crook and spent two years in jail.

SOUND-LETTER WORK 11.10 • LOOK, LISTEN, AND SAY

OO	UE	U..E	EW	OU
boot	due	lube	new	you
pool	sue	rude	blew	soup
cool	true	rule	threw	youth
tool	blue	tube	stew	route

AND: fruit suit shoe through who do to

SOUND-LETTER WORK 11.11 • READ AND SAY

pool	glue	fool	clue	stew	food	screw	tooth
crew	flew	slew	proof	toot	hoot	too	fruit
loot	lute	crude	you	shoe	ruler	Sue	due

SOUND-LETTER WORK 11.12 • READ

Mom: Who threw Sue's new shoes into the pool?

Sue: Ruth did.

Mom: Ruth? Did you do that?

Ruth: Sue pushed me into the pool.

Sue: Yeah, and then you grabbed my foot and pulled me in too. My blue swim suit got wet, and you knew I couldn't swim without my tube. That wasn't cool.

Mom: All right, kids, cool it! Let's not fool around at the pool. Look at the sign. It says, "Pool Rules. No pushing, no running, no jumping, no food in the pool." And now I say, "No fools at the pool." We're going home.

SOUND-LETTER WORK 11.13 • WRITE SENTENCES

Use some of the words in 11.7 and 11.11.

1. _____

2. _____

3. _____

4. _____

5. _____

 ## SOUND-LETTER WORK 11.14 • LISTEN AND WRITE

1 _____   2 _____   3 _____

4 _____   5 _____   6 _____

7 _____   8 _____   9 _____

10 _____

 ## SOUND-LETTER WORK 11.15 • LISTEN AND SAY

J j   G g

j – a – m	g – e – m	j – u – s – t	J – a – c – k
r – a – g – e	J – a – p – a – n	a – g – e	g – l – u – e
G – r – e – g	j – o – k – e – r	J – o – h – n	b – u – d – g – e – t

SOUND-LETTER WORK 11.16 • LISTEN AND WRITE

1 _____   2 _____   3 _____

4 _____   5 _____   6 _____

SOUND-LETTER WORK 11.17 • SPELL (SAY)

tooth	Grace	crew	German	jump
Greek	June	Jimmy	jot	jet

WORD WORK 11.1 • LISTEN AND SAY

WR	TW	TR
write	twin	trap
wrote	twine	trip
written	twice	train
wrong	twist	track
	BUT: two	

WORD WORK 11.2 • READ AND SAY

wrath	wrist	twenty	tree	twinkle	trestle
wrestle	tweed	treat	tweak	wreck	two

WORD WORK 11.3 • READ

Terry "the Wrecker" Wright is a wrestler. His twin brother, Tommy "Rat Trap" Wright is also a wrestler. They wrestle together as a tag team. They are the Wright Brothers. Last week they wrestled the Wrong Brothers, Two Ton Tweed and Teddy Twinkle Toes. The Wrights won when Terry twisted Two Ton's wrist and Tommy tripped Twinkle Toes, and then trapped him in a trestle hold.

 ## WORD WORK 11.4 • LISTEN AND SAY

(y)use   m(y)usic   h(y)uman
  unit   unite   united

WORD WORK 11.5 • READ AND SAY

mute   museum   muse
hue   Hugh   huge   humor   human
  few   furious   cute   curious

WORD WORK 11.6 READ

There was music at the museum last night. Curiously, there were only a few people there. Hugh Uman played a Debussy flute tune. Tomorrow he plays at the Community Union Hall It's a huge place. I hope the place is full. It could be a huge success for him and his music.

January	February	March
April	May	June
July	August	September
October	November	December

WORD WORK 11.8 READ

HOLIDAYS

January	February	March
New Year's Day Martin Luther King Jr.'s Birthday	Presidents' Day	
April	**May**	**June**
	Memorial Day	
July	**August**	**September**
Independence Day		Labor Day
October	**November**	**December**
Columbus Day	Veterans Day Thanksgiving	Christmas

HANDWRITING WORK 11.1 • LOOK

Jill   Kid   Obie   Todd

HANDWRITING WORK 11.2 • READ

joke   keg   oak   tear

jar   kiss   off   top

joke   skip   stop   locker

Jack   Kobe   Odaka   Tibet

QU SQU OU OW

SOUND-LETTER WORK 12.1 • LOOK, LISTEN, AND READ

QU		SQU
quit	quiet	square
quote	quake	squash
queen	queer	squeak
quite	quick	squid

SOUND-LETTER WORK 12.2 • READ

quip	equipment	quantity	quality	quarts	quarters
squeal	squaw	squirrel	equal	equality	equator
quench	question	require	inquire	acquire	acquit

SOUND-LETTER WORK 12.3 • READ

Little Quincy Quinn was being quite naughty and noisy. His mother told him to be quiet for one hour. She would give him a quarter and take him to see the animals at Farmer Squires' Petting Farm. He was quite quiet for almost an hour—not a peep or a squeak from him. So the Quinns took little Quincy to the petting farm.

Quincy bought a quart of animal food with his quarter. He had a wonderful time. He squeezed a little chick and almost squashed it. He picked up a little pig, and it squealed. He grabbed a duck, and it quacked. He held a chicken, and it squawked. He chased the quails, and they quickly escaped. He chased a squirrel, and it went up a tree. Quincy squealed with delight.

At last the Quinns went home, and the farm was quiet again. The animals asked Queenie the Cow to complain to Mister Squires. "If that kid comes back again, we're going to quit," she said.

Q Q Q Q

q q q q

SOUND-LETTER WORK 12.5 • WRITE A QUESTION WITH THESE WORDS

quit .. job _____

quiet .. mice _____

quite .. nice _____

cute .. squirrel _____

SOUND-LETTER WORK 12.6 • LISTEN AND WRITE

1 _____   2 _____   3 _____

4 _____   5 _____   6 _____

7 _____   8 _____   9 _____

10 _____

_____

OW	OU
now	out
cow	south
vow	foul
down	mouth
clown	our

SOUND-LETTER WORK 12.8 • READ AND SAY

plow	owl	vowel	towel	growl	frown
crown	drown	round	proud	clown	sour

sound   how now brown cow   bounce to the ounce   found a hound

the downtown crowd is loud   a pound of ground   loud mouth

SOUND-LETTER WORK 12.9 • READ

The town of Brownfield is down south. It is about two hours from the mouth of the Powow River and around three hundred miles south of the Powder Horn Mountains. The town was founded in 1869 by Uriah and Howard Brown.

It is said the Brown brothers drowned in Trout Creek in 1875. But their bodies were never found. Nowadays the downtown is very nice. There is a fountain surrounded by flowers, and some great places to eat and shop. There's the Common Ground, the Hound and Crown Town House, the Great Grounds Coffee Shop, the House of Sound and Song, and the Night Owl Book Shop.

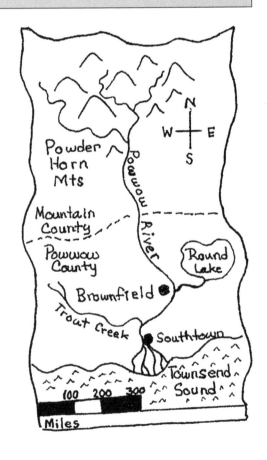

SOUND-LETTER WORK 12.10 • WRITE A SENTENCE WITH THESE WORDS

now _____

loud _____

pound _____

found _____

brown cow _____

plow _____

SOUND-LETTER WORK 12.11 • LISTEN AND WRITE

1 _____   2 _____   3 _____

4 _____   5 _____   6 _____

7 _____   8 _____   9 _____

10 _____

_____

SOUND-LETTER WORK 12.12 • LISTEN AND SAY

Q q	qu	squ
q – u – i – c – k	q – u – i – e – t	e – a – r – t – h – q – u – a – k – e
s – q – u – e – a – k	s – q – u – a – s – h	e – q – u – a – l

SOUND-LETTER WORK 12.13 • LISTEN AND WRITE

1 _____   2_____   3 _____

4 _____   5_____   6 _____

7 _____   8_____   9 _____

SOUND-LETTER WORK 12.14 • SPELL (SAY)

quit	squeak	quest	quart
quantity	squirrel	equator	square

WORD WORK 12.1 • LISTEN AND SAY

SK		SC	SCR
skid	ask	scat	scream
skip	task	scoop	screw
skate	risk	Scotland	scratch
ski	desk	scout	scramble
skull			

WORD WORK 12.2 • READ AND SAY

skin	scab	scrap	skill	score	scrape	scan	risk
screen	sky	scar	scrub	desk	skunk	scare	screech
sketch	scatter	ask	scoop	scope	escape	describe	prescribe

BUT: science   scissors

AND: school   scholar   schedule   scheme

So it's cold in Scandinavia. So what? In winter we ski on the snow and skate on the ice. It's nice. It's cool.

The radar scan shows only scattered snow showers, so let's skip school and go skiing and snowboarding.

Our science teacher scared us. She pulled a skull from a bag, and everybody screamed.

A bad scratch on the skin becomes a scab and then a scar.

scar: A scar is the result of an injury.

scare: To scare is to frighten or make afraid.

scrap: A scrap is a piece.

score: To score is to make a goal.

sketch: To sketch is to draw a picture.

skill: A skill is an ability.

skim: To skim is to look quickly.

scrub: To scrub is to wash very hard.

skunk: A skunk is an animal that smells bad.

GH

tough	rough	enough	cough
though	dough	through
caught	taught	thought	bought	ought	brought	sought

WORD WORK 12.6 • READ

Paul's cat taught her kittens to catch rats. Paul's cats caught a rat. They brought the rat to Paul. "Good," thought Paul, but then the cats brought more and more rats. "OK, enough!" said Paul. "Although I ought to be pleased, I don't know what to do with all these dead rats."

\WORD WORK12.7 • READ

Paula caught a cold. She coughed a lot. She coughed throughout the day. Although she had a rough night, she wouldn't take the cough medicine that Paul had bought. "You ought to take it," he said. In the morning her throat was very sore. "I hope that taught you a lesson," said Paul. "Don't try to be so tough."

HANDWRITING WORK 12.1 • LOOK

M m N n P p U u

Michelle Norman Paula Uriah

mope numb plum

HANDWRITING WORK 12.2 • READ

me need pound use

bump unit apple lump

Milan Nepal Paris Ukraine

UNIT 13   OY OI IR ER OR UR AR

SOUND-LETTER WORK 13.1 • LOOK, LISTEN, AND SAY

OY	OI
boy	oil
toy	toil
soy	soil
coy	coil

SOUND-LETTER WORK 13.2 • READ AND SAY

void	steroid	Troy	annoy	Roy	joy	oyster
boiler	foil	royal	destroy	Floyd	coin	boy
poison	employ	spoil	join	point	noise	avoid

SOUND-LETTER WORK 13.3 • READ

On the Croy Coast, two young boys were playing with their toys when they saw the boats come ashore. They ran to the city and told their story.

The Crojans were annoyed. Once more boats had come ashore on their soil. "Take this note," said His Royal Highness, the King of Croy. "And tell those folks to leave our shores, or we'll boil them in oil."

A note came back. "We're only oystermen from Soyland. We stop only to rest, taking a break from our toil. We will avoid any conflict with Croy."

And so the poet Roymer wrote the story of the Crojan Ploy, and how the Soylanders destroyed Croy with their gift of poisoned oysters.

1. Who saw the boats come ashore? _____

_____

2. How did the Crojans feel? _____

_____

3. Who said, "We'll boil them in oil?" _____

_____

4. Where were the oystermen from? _____

_____

5. Who wrote the story of the Crojan Ploy? _____

_____

6. How did the Soylanders destroy Croy? _____

_____

SOUND-LETTER WORK 13.5 • LISTEN AND WRITE

1 _____   2_____   3_____

4 _____   5_____   6_____

7 _____   8_____   9_____

10 _____

SOUND-LETTER WORK 13.6 • LOOK, LISTEN, AND SAY

UR	OR	ER	IR
spur	word	verb	bird
blur	worth	herd	third
hurt	worse	defer	flirt
absurd	work	Herb	squirt

AND: heard earth earn   **BUT:** ear hear   **AND:** sure

SOUND-LETTER WORK 13.7 • READ AND SAY

nerd	curd	shirt	world	absurd	flirt	sailor	worry	urge
worm	worse	curb	murderer	work	Serb	sir	blurt	stir
spur	smirk	squirt	certain	surf	surface	hurt	spurt	fur

SOUND-LETTER WORK 13.8 • READ

Ernie and Bertha are worriers. They worry a lot. They worry about their work. They worry about the world. They worry about the weather. They think it's getting worse. They're sure the world is warming up. They believe that the surface of the earth is drying up. They think that animals will lose their fur. They worry that the birds won't find worms. They think the heat will hurt the turtles. They heard about a survey that showed a third of the great herds of African animals have disappeared.

 SOUND-LETTER WORK 13.9 • LOOK, LISTEN, AND SAY

			AR				
car	bar	tar	hard	card	art	part	park
par	far	are	cart	mart	large	barge	yard

bard	lard	Bart	dart	tart	arm	farm	harm	darn
yarn	carp	tarp	harp	ark	lark	hark	mark	car

SOUND-LETTER WORK 13.11 • READ

Did you know that poets
Are also known as bards?
And bards can sing like birds?
Shakespeare wrote these words:
"Hark, hark, the lark."
And Wordsworth was a poet.
Did you know it?
He wrote about a bird,
A bird that he heard.
He heard it in a park,
He heard it in the dark,
He heard it in his yard,
And he heard it on a farm,
And so he went to work.

Starting with a verb,
He wrote from his heart,
And the bird that he heard
Was also a lark.

SOUND-LETTER WORK 13.12 • LISTEN AND WRITE

1 _____   2 _____   3 _____

4 _____   5 _____   6 _____

7 _____   8 _____   9 _____

10 _____

_____

WORD WORK 13.1 • LISTEN AND SAY

WH

when	whether	which	whale	where
wheel	while	what	why	

WORD WORK 13.2 • READ AND SAY

wheat   whip   whisper   whistle   whiskey   white

WORD WORK 13.3 • READ

All day at sea, and not a single sighting of a gray whale. "One last look," she said as she picked up the glasses and scanned to the east. Suddenly, "Whale!" she whispered.

"Where?" he whispered back.

"There," she pointed. He saw the spout and whistled in disbelief. It must be huge. He grabbed the wheel and whipped the little boat about, heading straight for the spout.

"Which kind?" he asked.

"I'm not sure. I can't tell whether it's a gray or a humpback, but I don't think it's gray. Suddenly, she dropped the glasses and knocked over the bottle of whiskey.

"What's wrong?" And then he, too, saw it rise out of the sea and head straight for them — the Great White Whale!

 WORD WORK 13.4 • LISTEN AND SAY

PH

Philadelphia	phone	physical	graph	Ralph
phantom	pharmacy	phase	pheasant	phenomenal
phonetic	photograph	phrase	phonics	triumph

Phil	physics	telephone	grapheme	phase
philosopher	phonics	photo	phrase	physical

WORD WORK 13.6 • READ

Phil, Ralph, and Phyllis are friends. They are students at Philadelphia University. Phil is majoring in physics. He wants to be a physicist. Phyllis is studying medicine. She wants to go to Phillips Medical College and become a physician. Ralph doesn't know what he wants. He loves photography, and when he was a sophomore he got a trophy for a photograph he took in the Philippine Islands. But you can't major in photography at PU. He's thinking about pharmacy, and maybe physical therapy, but he just took a course in phonetics, and he liked it a lot. But what does a phonetician do?

 WORD WORK 13.7 • LISTEN AND SAY

SPR	STR	SW	SM	SPL
spring	string	swing	smoke	spleen
sprung	strung	swung	smack	split
spray	stray	sway	smell	splendid

WORD WORK 13.8 • READ AND SAY

sprayed	splash	splint	stripe	swipe	smite
sweet	street	spread	sweat	small	strong
swim	sprain	stream	smile	strike	display
swell	straight	smash	strip	smart	swift

Dear Mom and Dad,

    I'm having a swell time with Skip, Phil, and Uncle Steve. Last week we hiked for seven straight days in the Smoky Mountains National Park. At the end of the first day we were hot and sweaty, and we camped by a river. We couldn't swim because the current was very swift—it was too strong for swimming. But we splashed around and had fun.

    On the second day it sprinkled a little, but it really didn't rain hard.

    On the third day we had lots of fun splashing around in a small stream, but suddenly a thunderstorm hit us. Lightning struck all around us. It was a little scary and stressful. A big spruce tree crashed down near us.

    On the fourth day we strayed off the trail a little and got lost in a swamp. Skip got stuck in a big hole and almost got swallowed up. Uncle Steve got a strap from his pack and pulled him out.

    On the fifth day Phil found a strange little baby animal. It was really cute with black and white stripes. Skip didn't know it was a skunk. He started to chase it, but it lifted its tail and sprayed Phil. He smelled awful.

    On the sixth day Skip strained his back, so he and I swapped packs because his was too heavy. But that part of the trail wasn't smooth at all, and I sprained my ankle. Uncle Steve had to carry most of the stuff in my pack.

    On the seventh day we came down off the mountain. There were lots of switchbacks in the trail. Phil fell and smashed into a big rock. He banged his knee so Uncle Steve had to carry most of the stuff in Phil's pack. Uncle Steve swore a lot, but when we finally got to the end of the trail, he smiled a little and said, "That was a splendid trip, wasn't it, guys?"

    We were going to spend a few more days hiking, but for some strange reason we're staying at Uncle Steve's camp on Swan Pond, and Uncle Steve is sleeping all the time.

                    Roy

zero   point   degree   Fahrenheit   Celcius   centimeter   inch

kilometer   tenth   mile   percent   half   quarter

202 (Two-oh-two is also two-zero-two.)   2.5 (two point five)

2.2   98.6   0.62   3.14159   0.9

32 degrees Fahrenheit is 0 degrees Celsius.

212° F is 100° C.

1 centimeter equals 0.39 inches.

1 kilometer equals six-tenths of a mile.

50 percent is one-half of 100.

25% is one-quarter of 100.

1/4   1/3   1/2

NUMBER WORK 13.2 READ AND SAY

1.1   2.54   1.609   0.964   2.1   0.39   99.9   0.035

50°F is 10°C.   32.2°C = 90°F.   90%   60%

NUMBER WORK 13.3 READ

80%   75°   91.7%   5°   0.5%   32°F   15°C   4.25%

20°C is 68°F.   80°F is 26.7°C.   33% is one-third.

10% is one-tenth.   50% is one-half.   25% is one-quarter.

One mile = 1.609 kilometers.   1/10 = 0.1

Qq Vv Ww

Quentin Victor Walter

quit vase will

quiet equal wave verb

Quentin waited for Walter.

Victor saw William in Quebec.

UNIT 14   # X Z ZZ

 SOUND-LETTER WORK 14.1 LOOK, LISTEN, AND SAY

X

Max	tax	taxi	Tex	Rex	sex	hex	ox	pox	lox
sox	six	sax	axe	mix	nix	tux	next	exit	toxic

SOUND-LETTER WORK 14.2 • READ AND SAY

tax	sex	Mexico	Texas	lexical	excellent
fix	mix	maximum	sixty	box	smallpox

 SOUND-LETTER WORK 14.3 • LOOK, LISTEN, AND SAY

Z   ZZ

zap	haze	buzz	size	lazy	zoo
jazz	crazy	daze	razz	zen	dizzy

SOUND-LETTER WORK 14.4 • READ AND SAY

raze	size	haze	froze	freeze
breeze	lazy	dizzy	Zack	Zoey

SOUND-LETTER WORK 14.5 • READ

doze	crazy	hex	lazy	maze	lax	zone
zest	mixie	zebra	zero	Roxanne	zoom	size
freeze	sixteen	Zack	razor	mixed	fuzzy	breeze

142 ● FROM SOUND TO SENTENCE

Max Zizza loves music, movies, and the zoo. Friday evening after work he goes to Zero's Jazz shack to hear Dizzy Bix play the sax. On Saturday Max walks to the Rex Cinema to see a film. Last Saturday he saw Tex Baxter in an exciting western, "The Dirty Dozen in Mexico." Next Saturday he's going to see Zack Zeno and Zoey Sexton in "The Frozen Zone."

On Sunday Max walks six blocks to Roxy's Deli for his usual bagel and lox brunch. Then he takes the taxi for an exciting day at the zoo. On his first stop he watches the busy, crazy chimps. Then he looks at the lazy snakes. His favorite animal is the zebra, although he also likes the zebu and the musk ox.

At the bird house he watches the buzzards. Last on his walk is his friend the fox (Max has a thing about "X" and "Z"). Max talks to the fox, and the fox gazes at Max and hopes that some day Max will put him in a box, sneak out the exit, and let him go to be free like the breeze.

X X X X

x x x x

Z Z Z Z Z

z z z z z

What kind of music does Max like? _____

_____

Who plays the sax at the Jazz Shack? _____

_____

What does Max eat on Sunday morning? _____

_____

How does Max get to the zoo? _____

_____

What is Max's favorite animal? _____

_____

1 _____ 2 _____ 3 _____

4 _____ 5 _____ 6 _____

7 _____ 8 _____ 9 _____

10 _____

X x   Z z

b – o – x	w – a – x	z – o – o	m – a – z – e
t – a – x – i	j – a – z – z	T – e – x	Z – e – k – e

1 _____ 2 _____ 3 _____

4 _____ 5 _____ 6 _____

SOUND-LETTER WORK 14.12 • SPELL (SAY)

zip	mix	next	zeal	zoo
daze	dozen	breeze	wax	zone

The Craziest Language

We'll begin with a box and the plural is boxes;
But the plural of ox should be oxen, not oxes.
Then one fowl is goose, but two are called geese,
Yet the plural of moose should never be meese.
You may find a lone mouse or a nest full of mice;
Yet the plural of house is houses, not hice.
If the plural of man is always called men,
Why shouldn't the plural of pan be pen?
If I spoke of my foot and showed you my feet,
Then I show you two boots, why aren't they called beet?
Well, the masculine pronouns are he, his, and him.
But imagine the feminine she, shis, and shim.
So English I fancy you will agree,
Is the craziest language you ever did see.

X x   Y y   Z z
X-ray   Yanni   Zeke
fax   way   zoo

zone   crazy   taxi   eye

Yesterday Zeke took a taxi to the jazz festival.

The quick brown fox jumped over the lazy dog.

We the People of the United States,
in order to form a more perfect Union,
establish Justice, insure domestic Tranquility,
provide for the common Defense,
promote the general Welfare,
and secure the Blessings of Liberty
to ourselves and our Posterity,
do ordain and establish this Constitution
for the United States of America.

ATLANTA

POPULATION: 416,474

    WHITE: 33.2 percent

    BLACK: 61.4%

    HISPANIC: 4.5%

    ASIAN: 1.9%

WEATHER

    AVG JAN TEMP: 41.0 degrees

    AVG JULY TEMP: 78.8°F

Atlanta is the largest city and capital of Georgia. It is situated in the northern part of the state at the base of the Blue Ridge Mountains.

BOSTON

POPULATION: 589,141

    WHITE: 54.5 percent

    BLACK: 25.3%

    HISPANIC: 14.4%

    ASIAN: 7.5%

WEATHER

    AVG JAN TEMP: 28.6 degrees

    AVG JULY TEMP: 73.5°F

Boston is the capital of and largest city in Massachusetts. It is in the eastern part of the state on Massachusetts Bay. It was settled in 1623.

CHICAGO

POPULATION: 2,896,016

    WHITE: 42 percent

    BLACK: 36.8%

    HISPANIC: 26%

    ASIAN: 4.3%

WEATHER

    AVG JAN TEMP: 22.4 degrees

    AVG JULY TEMP: 75.1°F

Chicago is the largest city in Illinois. It is the seat of Cook County. It is on the southwest shore of Lake Michigan.

DALLAS

POPULATION: 1,188,580

    WHITE: 50.8 percent

    BLACK: 25.9%

    HISPANIC: 35.6%

    ASIAN: 2.7%

WEATHER

    AVG JAN TEMP: 44.6 degrees

    AVG JULY TEMP: 85.9°F

Dallas is the second largest city in Texas. It is 185 miles northeast of Austin, the capital of Texas. It is located on the Trinity River.

DENVER

POPULATION: 554,636

    WHITE: 65.3 percent

    BLACK: 11.1%

    HISPANIC: 31.7%

    ASIAN: 1%

WEATHER

    AVG JAN TEMP: 29.7 degrees

    AVG JULY TEMP: 73.5°F

Denver is the largest city in Colorado. It is also the capital of Colorado. It is situated at the foot of the Rocky Mountains.

DETROIT

POPULATION: 951,270

    WHITE: 12.3 percent

    BLACK: 81.6%

    HISPANIC: 5%

    ASIAN: 1%

WEATHER

    AVG JAN TEMP: 24.7 degrees

    AVG JULY TEMP: 74.2°F

Detroit is the largest city in Michigan. It is in the southeast part of the state. It is on the Detroit River. It shares the river with Canada.

HOUSTON

POPULATION: 1,953,631
- WHITE: 49.3 percent
- BLACK: 25.3%
- HISPANIC: 37.4%
- ASIAN: 5.3%

WEATHER
- AVG JAN TEMP: 52.2 degrees
- AVG JULY TEMP: 83.5°F

Houston is the largest city in Texas. It is the seat of Harris County. It is located in the southeastern part of the state near the Gulf of Mexico.

KANSAS CITY

POPULATION
- WHITE: 60.7%
- BLACK: 31.2%
- HISPANIC: 6.9%
- ASIAN: 1.9%
- AMERINDIAN:0.5%

WEATHER
- AVG JAN TEMP: 25.7 degrees
- AVG JULY TEMP: 78.5° F

Kansas City is the largest city in Missouri. Part of the city is in the state of Kansas. It is at the junction of the Missouri and Kansas Rivers. It is named after the Kansa Indians.

LOS ANGELES

POPULATION: 3,694,820
- WHITE: 46.9 percent
- BLACK: 11.2%
- HISPANIC: 46.5%
- ASIAN: 10%

WEATHER
- AVG JAN TEMP: 58.3 degrees
- AVG JULY TEMP: 74.3°F

Los Angeles is the largest city in California and second-largest in the US. It is located in southern California on the Pacific Ocean. It is a very important port.

MIAMI

POPULATION: 362,470
- WHITE: 66.6 percent
- BLACK: 22.3%
- HISPANIC: 65.8%
- ASIAN: 0.7%

WEATHER
- AVG JAN TEMP: 67.2 degrees
- AVG JULY TEMP: 82.6°F

Miami is the seat of Miami-Dade County. It is the second largest city in Florida. It is in the southeast on Biscayne Bay. The Bay is part of the Atlantic Coast.

MINNEAPOLIS

POPULATION: 382,618
- WHITE: 65.1%
- BLACK: 18%
- HISPANIC: 7.6%
- ASIAN: 6.1%
- AMERINDIAN: 2.2%

WEATHER
- AVG JAN TEMP: 11.8 degrees
- AVG JULY TEMP: 73.6° F

Minneapolis is the largest city in Minnesota. It is located on the Mississippi River. Its neighbor, St. Paul, is the capital of Minnesota. The two cities are often called "The Twin Cities."

NEW YORK

POPULATION: 8,008,278
- WHITE: 44.7 percent
- BLACK: 26.6%
- HISPANIC: 27%
- ASIAN: 9.8%

WEATHER
- AVG JAN TEMP: 31.5 degrees
- AVG JULY TEMP: 76.8°F

New York is the largest city in the US. It is in the southern part of New York State on the Hudson River. It is the busiest port in the United States.

PHILADELPHIA
POPULATION: 1,517,550
>WHITE: 45 percent
>BLACK: 43.2%
>HISPANIC: 8.5%
>ASIAN: 4.5%

WEATHER
>AVG JAN TEMP: 30.4 degrees
>AVG JULY TEMP: 76.7°F

Philadelphia is a city and a county. It is the largest city in Pennsylvania. It is located in southeastern Pennsylvania at the junction of the Schuylkill and Delaware Rivers.

PHOENIX
POPULATION: 1,321,095
>WHITE: 71.1 percent
>BLACK: 5.1%
>HISPANIC: 34.1%
>ASIAN: 2%
>AMERINDIAN: 2%

WEATHER
>AVG JAN TEMP: 53.6 degrees
>AVG JULY TEMP: 93.5°F

Phoenix is the largest city in Arizona. It is the seat of Maricopa County, and it is in the center of the state on the Salt River.

SAN DIEGO
POPULATION: 1,223,400
>WHITE: 60.2 percent
>BLACK: 7.9%
>HISPANIC: 25.4%
>ASIAN: 13.6%

WEATHER
>AVG JAN TEMP: 57.4 degrees
>AVG JULY TEMP: 71°F

San Diego is the second largest city in California. It is located in the southwest part of the state on San Diego Bay, part of the Pacific Ocean.

SAN FRANCISCO
POPULATION: 776,733
>WHITE: 49.7 percent
>BLACK: 7.8%
>HISPANIC: 14.1%
>ASIAN: 30.8%

WEATHER
>AVG JAN TEMP: 51.1 degrees
>AVG JULY TEMP: 59.1°F

San Francisco is the fourth largest city in the state of California. It is both a city and a county. It is located on San Francisco Bay, on the Pacific Ocean coast.

SEATTLE
POPULATION: 563,374
>WHITE: 70.1 percent
>BLACK: 8.4%
>HISPANIC: 5.3%
>ASIAN: 13.1%
>AMERINDIAN: 1%

WEATHER
>AVG JAN TEMP: 40.1 degrees
>AVG JULY TEMP: 65.2°F

Seattle is the largest city in Washington State. It is between Puget Sound and Lake Washington in the northeastern part of the state. It is one of the major ports of the United States.

WASHINGTON, D.C.
POPULATION: 572,059
>WHITE: 30.8 percent
>BLACK: 60%
>HISPANIC: 7.9%
>ASIAN: 2.7%

WEATHER
>AVG JAN TEMP: 34.6 degrees
>AVG JULY TEMP: 80°F

The city of Washington is also the federal District of Columbia. It is the capital of the United States. It is between the states of Virginia and Maryland on the Potomac River.

TOWN PARKS DEPARTMENT
SPRING NEWSLETTER

CHECK US OUT AT OUR WEB SITE www.town.org

Girls Softball Registration
When: Tuesday, March 22, 3:30–6 p.m.
Where: Youth Center Conference Room
Ages: Girls in grades 3 through 6
Parent information sheets will be available

Little League Baseball Registration
When: Thursday, March 24, 4–6 p.m.
Where: Community Center
Ages: Boys and girls born between 8/1/92 and
    7/31/97
Cost: $20 resident/$35 nonresident
Birth certificates are required at registration

Gymnastics Registration
When: Friday, April 8, 3:30 p.m.
Where: Gibson Middle School
Ages: 3 & up, co-ed, (6-week session)
Classes begin week of April 9
Cost: $37.50 resident/$52.50 nonresident
Instructor: Meg Jackson

Easter Egg Hunt
When: Saturday, March 26
Time: 9:30 a.m.—ages 3 & under
    9:45 a.m.—ages 4 to 6
    10 a.m.—ages 7 & up
Where: Memorial Park
There will be four stuffed animal prizes in each
    age group. Each child needs to have a basket
    or container to collect the eggs.

Splish, Splash & Swim
When: Monday, April 18, 11 a.m.–1 p.m.
Where: West Side Spa and Health Center
Cost: $3 children/$5 adults
Under 7 must be with an adult
Long hair must be braided or in a swim cap
Preregister at 257-5890

Super Bike and Fun Day
When: April 22, 10:30–noon
Activities: 10:30—Bike rodeo (helmets required)
    —inspection and registration by Town Police
        Department
    —safety talk by Captain Brown, State
        Police Department
Where: Memorial Park. In case of rain the event
    will be held in the Wilson Skating Rink

Youth Lacrosse
When: Saturdays, April 9–May 21
Time: 9:30 a.m.–10:30 a.m.—girls
10:45 a.m.–11:45 a.m.—boys
Ages: Grades 5 through 8
Cost: $25 resident/$40 nonresident
Instructors: Jill Parker and Sam Mayberry

Bowling Day
When: Tuesday, April 19, 10 a.m.–2 p.m.
Where: Bowladrome, 225 County Road
Ages: 7–15, under 7 must be with an adult
Cost: $6.75–includes 2 games, shoes, a hot dog,
    & a soda

BIG MOUNTAIN COUNTY CALENDAR
September 30–October 1, 2006

SATURDAY

DANCE: 7–11 p.m. Moose Hall, 570 N. Main Street, Bridgeton. Sponsor: Big Mountain Dance and Social Club. Band: Country Hearts. Contra and line dancing. Refreshments served. Members $6; nonmembers $8.

THEATER: The Actors Playhouse, corner of Brook and Main Street, Center Brownfield. *Twelve Angry Men* 8 p.m. All seats $10. Final performance. "Great": Bill Oldberg, drama critic, *County News*. Reservations: 257-5097.

KIDS: Annie's music and puppets performance. Kidzplayce, 15 Flat Street, Evansburg. Original children's music and handmade puppets. Donations welcome. Sponsored by Evansburg Parents Club and Town Recreation Department.

CLEANUP: East River Cleanup Day, 9:30 a.m. Meet at the Stoneville Bridge on East River. Bring gloves. Bags provided. Come help clean the river in Mountain County. Part of the annual Mountains to Mouth Cleanup sponsored by Great Rivers Society.

FOOD: Ham and bean supper, 5–8:30 p.m. Community Church, Brownfield. Menu: baked beans, hot dogs, macaroni and cheese, coleslaw, rolls, and homemade pies. Adults $7; children under 12, $4. First seating 5 p.m.; second seating 7 p.m.

FLEA MARKET: 8:30 a.m.–4 p.m. Evansburg Common. Chinaware, silverware, pots, pans, glass items, tools, toys, books, bake sale, more. Sponsored by Evansburg Ladies Civic Club. Benefit: Town Recreation Program. Donations accepted until August 28.

SUNDAY

MUSIC/DANCE: Native American Festival, 2–4 p.m. Big Mountain Town Hall. Watch tribal dancing by Powwow Indian dancers and drummers. Sponsored by Bridgeton Folklore Club. Potluck; bring refreshments to share. Info: 279-6657.

HIKE: Eagle Mountain Outdoor Club. Hike to Eagle Falls. Easy hike, 4–5 miles. Last half-mile steep. Bring snack, lunch, water. Good walking shoes recommended. Bring glasses for birding. Guide: Bill Wallace. Meet at Eagle Mountain State park, 9 a.m.

RIVERSIDE COUNTY FAIR AND DATE FESTIVAL, Indio, California, northeast of San Diego, February. The Coachella Valley produces 35 million pounds of dates every year. Walk through the shady date palm garden. Check out the more than 7,000 exhibits. Sample more than 50 different kinds of dates. Lots of entertainment. Almost 300,000 people attended in 2006. www.datefest.org

WORLD CATFISH FESTIVAL. Belzoni, Mississippi, April. Humphreys County in west-central Mississippi is called the "Catfish Capital of the World." Entertainment. Miss Catfish pageant. The world's largest catfish fry. Try the fried catfish, hush puppies, and coleslaw dinner. Enter the catfish-eating contest. www.catfishcapitalonline.com

VIDALIA ONION FESTIVAL. Vidalia, Georgia. April. The Vidalia onion is a mild, sweet onion. It is grown only in a 20-county area of Georgia. Enjoy the onion cook-off and tasting. Try them raw or as deep-fried onion rings. Tour local farms. Watch the air show. Lots of music and sidewalk sales. www.vidaliaga.com

STOCKTON ASPARAGUS FESTIVAL. Stockton, California, April. Voted one of the best food festivals in the West. Taste the best, fresh asparagus. Strolling entertainment—puppets and stilts. Watch the deep-fried eating contest. 40,000 pounds of asparagus are cooked and eaten. www.asparagusfest.com

GREAT WISCONSIN CHEESE FESTIVAL. Little Chute, Wisconsin, June. Near Appleton and Green Bay. The celebration of cheese includes music, food, games, rides, and an animal petting zoo. And of course, lots of cheese. Look at the cheese carvings. Enjoy the cheese tasting, cheesecake competition, and cheese curds. www.littlechutewi.org/calendar_events/cheesefest.html

PINK TOMATO FESTIVAL. Warren, Arkansas, June. Local people call their tomatoes "the world's tastiest tomato." They may not look ripe, but that's because they are pink when they are ready to eat. Try them at the festival. There's a tomato-eating contest, a salsa competition, the Miss Pink Tomato Contest, and an all-tomato lunch. www.bradleycountychamberofcommerce.com

FISH, FOLK, AND FUN FESTIVAL. Twillingate, Newfoundland, July. Enjoy our beautiful coastline. Watch the whales and the icebergs from the Arctic and join our culture and heritage celebration. We have music, dancing, and our traditional meals with cod, salmon, and lobster. www.fishfunfolkfestival.com

SPRINGFIELD FILBERT FESTIVAL. Springfield, Oregon, August. The Willamette Valley produces 99% of America's filberts (also called hazelnuts). Try filberts spiced, roasted, or chocolate-covered. Kids will love the Nutty Kingdom Play Area. You'll like the ice cream social and live music on two stages. www.springfieldfilbertfestival.com

BLACKBERRY FESTIVAL. Powell River, British Columbia, August. The people of Powell River on British Columbia's Sunshine Coast celebrate the sweet, black berries with a street party, street musicians, clowns, and lots of blackberries. Cooking contest for desserts. Try blackberry pie or blackberry dessert pizza. www.discoverpowellriver.com

NATIONAL LENTIL FESTIVAL. Pullman, Washington, August. The lentil is an ancient cousin of the bean. It is very nutritious. One-third of all the lentils grown in the U.S. are grown in eastern Washington and northern Idaho. Celebrate the lentil with a lentil pancake breakfast, a parade, a cook-off, a 5K fun run/walk, games, a food court, and a street fair. www.lentilfest.com

NORFOLK WATERMELON FESTIVAL. Norfolk, Nebraska, August. Northeastern Nebraska produces lots of sweet, juicy watermelons. At the festival there are arts and crafts exhibits, pony rides, carnival games, watermelon-eating contests, a classic car show, and a seed-spitting contest. www.norfolk.ne.us/tourism.

IDAHO SPUD DAY. Shelley, Idaho, September. Bingham County is the top potato-growing county in the U.S. The annual festival celebrates the potato with a parade, music, a baked potato cook-off, a free baked potato lunch, a potato-picking contest and mashed potato wrestling as part of the Great Potato Games. www.visitidaho .org/thingstodo/events.aspx?eventid=3900

PIG-PICKIN' CHICKEN LICKIN' FEAST. Independence, Missouri, September. A great feast of roast pork, fried chicken, and all the trimmings. It's all on the grounds of the Bingham-Waggoner Estate under black walnut trees. Silent auctions, tours of the home and live music by the Kansas City Banjo Band. www.ci.independence.mo.us/userdocs/tourism/

BARNESVILLE PUMPKIN FESTIVAL. Barnesville, Ohio, September. Fun for all. At the fall festival treat yourself to pumpkin pancakes, pumpkin fudge, or a pumpkin shake. Participate in the pumpkin-pushing race. Check out the King Pumpkin contest. Winners are often more than 1,000 pounds. Homemade goods, classic cars, recipes, and more. www.pumpkinfestival.8k.com

NAPLES GRAPE FESTIVAL. Naples, New York, September. Try a grape pie at the "Grape Pie Capital of the World" in the Finger Lakes Region. 80,000 visitors. 20,000 pies. International food. Entertainment tents. Grape Pie Cooking Contest. Take off your shoes and enter the Grape Stompin' Contest. www.naplesvalleyny.com/grapefest.php

CLAREMORE BLUEGRASS AND CHILI FESTIVAL. Claremore, Oklahoma, September. A great weekend of family fun. Three stages of free entertainment. Arts and crafts, open car show, dance exhibition, quilt show, food and beverages, and the Mid-America Regional Chili Cook-Off. No coolers. Bring lawn chairs. www.claremore.org/bluegrass_chili_festival.htm

PEMAQUID OYSTER FESTIVAL.
Damariscotta, Maine, September. The Sunday
festival opens at noon and closes at dusk, rain or
shine. Entertainment, educational exhibits, boat
rides to the oyster beds in the Damariscotta
River. And lots of oysters. 8,000 served fresh on
the half shell, stewed, broiled, or baked.
www.mainelincolncountynews.com/
index.cfm?ID=21356

THE WHOLE ENCHILADA FIESTA. Las
Cruces, New Mexico, September. One of the
largest events in New Mexico is a celebration of
Southwestern culture, food, and history. Watch
the making of the world's largest enchilada.
Enjoy the vendors, the parade, the bands, classic
cars, and many more events. Over 70,000 people
attend the three-day event, now more than 20
years old. Dona_Ana/LasCruces/
TheWholeEnchiladaFestival.htm

TASTE OF NEWARK. Newark, Delaware,
October. Sample food from 40 restaurants. Try
the wine and beer from 15 local wineries and
microbreweries. Enjoy live entertainment and a
silent auction on the grounds of the University
of Delaware. newark.de.us/downtown/taste-of
-newark.htm

NORSK HØSTFEST. Minot, North Dakota,
October. This is North America's largest Scandi-
navian festival. Try lute-fisk (cod), lefske,
Swedish meatballs, Danish Kringle. Enjoy arts
and crafts from Denmark, Finland, Iceland,
Norway, and Sweden. Enjoy yodelers, folk
dancers, and lots of famous entertainers.
www.hostfest.com

CHATSWORTH CRANBERRY FESTIVAL.
Chatsworth, New Jersey, October. New Jersey
has the third-largest harvest of cranberries. Tour
the cranberry bogs in a tour bus. Enjoy the native
North American fruit as cranberry sauce, cranberry mustard, vinegar, ice cream, juice, bread,
and cake. Artists, antiques, classic cars. Free
admission.
www.cranfest.org

DUMMERSTON APPLE PIE FESTIVAL.
Dummerston Center, Vermont, October. For
more than 40 years the folks of Dummerston
have baked and sold over 1,500 apple pies. Also
enjoy hot or cold apple cider, Vermont cheddar
cheese, donuts, and ice cream. Shop for books,
crafts, and treasures at the Grange. Attend the
firemen's pancake breakfast.
www.dummerston.com

POPCORN FESTIVAL OF CLAY COUNTY.
Brazil, Indiana, October. This three-day festival
has something for everyone. Pottery, soap-
making, a snack foods tent, a laser light show,
fireworks, classic cars, the flying K9s—
professional dog disc catchers. And of course,
a popcorn-eating contest and free popcorn for
everyone. www.popcornfest.net

KONA COFFEE CULTURAL FESTIVAL.
Kailua Kona, Hawaii, November. Attend the
festival in the only state where coffee is grown
commercially. Watch coffee brewers at work in
the Cupping Contest. Try picking some beans.
Sample the different blends. Try a coffee dessert.
Parade, concert, and the Miss Kona Coffee
Scholarship Pageant at Hawaii's oldest food
festival. www.konacoffeefest.com

SLW 1.11

Ed	Dad	Ted
Deb	Pat	dip
bad	bit	bed
tab	pit	tip

SLW 1.14

b-a-d	p-e-t	d-i-p
b-e-t	b-i-t	p-a-d
b-a-t	d-i-d	b-e-d

NW 1.4

2	4	3	0	5	1
T3	P4	I5	B1	2D	1A
A201		B324		E251	
1352		4130		5240	
254-3012		321-5410		415-3202	
512-413-2100		212-354-1534			

SLW 2.9

sit	pats	beds
steps	dabs	stab
sad	best	pits
test	stat	stet

SLW 2.11

s-i-t-s	p-a-s-t	s-t-e-p
p-i-t-s	t-e-s-t	d-a-d-s
p-a-s-t	s-i-p	b-e-s-t

NW 2.4

7	9	65	8	10	00
B8	P7	D6	E9	S6	A10
7D		8B		I9	10C
701		963		586	794
10-6-85		2-7-37		9-6-89	
217-6997		480-6839		708-1967	

SLW 3.11

1. Ben	2. Dan	3. Don	4. Pam
5. spot	6. boss	7. snip	8. spin
	9. bass	10. snob	

SLW 3.13

1. m-o-m	2. s-a-n-d	3. m-e-s-s
4. d-i-m	5. m-a-p	6. p-o-n-d
7. s-t-o-p	8. p-o-t	9. s-p-i-n

NW 3.6

11	13	15	12	14	10
15	14	12	13	10	11
S12	P14		D15	T13	
11A	14S		13B	12E	
12:01	11:15		10:13	12:14	
11:15 a.m.	12:14 p.m.	10:13 p.m.	12:15 a.m.		

SLW 4.12

1. Brad	2. Bill	3. Bud
4. slap	5. plan	6. blast
7. drop	8. prep	9. dump
10. spun	11. slump	12. spell

SLW 4.14

1. t-u-b	2. l-a-m-p	3. s-l-u-m
4. s-u-n	5. r-e-s-t	6. b-r-a-t
7. d-r-u-m	8. b-u-s	9. l-i-s-t

NW 4.6

19	20	16	18	17
R17	L16	U20	S19	I18
26	29	23	25	
1917	1815	1620	1812	
1720	1916	1817	1920	
1724	1627	1822	1928	

SLW 5.14

1. landed	2. better	3. stepped
4. missed	5. dinner	6. rested
7. planned	8. dusted	9. speller
10. sobbed	11. batted	12. tossed

13. Beth, this is not the best path to the pond.

SLW 5.16

1. m-a-t-h
2. t-h-i-s
3. o-t-h-e-r
4. s-i-s-t-e-r
5. l-e-t-t-e-r
6. b-r-o-t-h-e-r
7. r-e-s-t-e-d
8. d-u-s-t-e-d
9. p-l-a-n-n-e-d

NW 5.5

40	60	90	30
50	70	80	20
93	87	36	44
59	75	62	21

R1.10

1. Brad
2. Beth
3. stand
4. pond
5. dropped
6. pest
7. blend
8. spot
9. lump
10. missed
11. bumped
12. tested

SLW 6.12

1. glass
2. crack
3. grab
4. gum
5. clip
6. rock
7. truck
8. cop
9. killed
10. Dick kissed Meg. Then Meg grabbed Dick's neck and slugged him.

SLW 6.14

1. c-u-p
2. k-i-d
3. c-a-n
4. p-i-g
5. p-i-c-k
6. l-o-c-k
7. g-l-a-d
8. g-r-u-b
9. c-r-a-c-k

NW 6.3

A. 59	B. 47	C. 28	D. 99
E. 100	F. 590	G. 129	H. 750
I. 205	J. 530	K. 770	L. 365
M. 1,760	N. 2,000	O. 2,050	P. 4,990
Q. 6,000	R. 15,470	S. 14,880	T. 13,313
U. 18,100	V. 16,640	W. 15,470	X. 14,480
	Y. 3,000,000	Z. 2,000,000,000	

SLW 7.7

1. Chuck
2. Hal
3. shock
4. hill
5. catch
6. dish
7. chest
8. pitcher
9. rush
10. Chuck had chicken for lunch at Chet's Chicken Hut
    and shellfish for dinner at Hal's Clam Shack.

SLW 7.13

1. cake
2. played
3. pay
4. paid
5. rain
6. ate
7. claim
8. gray
9. name

10. In May, Ray stayed eight rainy days in Spain.

SLW 7.15

1. h-a-s
2. h-a-y
3. e-a-c-h
4. s-u-c-h
5. p-i-t-c-h
6. S-p-a-i-n

SLW 8.5

1. dream
2. muddy
3. cheap
4. seat
5. heat
6. keep
7. sheep
8. these
9. sheet

10. Kathy seems sleepy. Did she eat a big meal?

SLW 8.12

1. cry
2. sight
3. dime
4. lie
5. try
6. nine
7. time
8. right
9. sky

10. Last night Mike and I dined on ripe lime pie.

SLW 8.14

1. f-e-e-l
2. h-i-g-h
3. s-l-e-e-p
4. t-r-y
5. d-i-m-e
6. p-l-e-a-s-e

SLW 9.5

1. Cindy
2. cent
3. city
4. space
5. lice
6. cell
7. mice
8. either
9. price

10. Candy put the citrus and spice in a nice place in the cellar.

SLW 9.15

1. fame
2. funny
3. drive
4. fight
5. save
6. veal
7. give
8. flying
9. vest

10. Frank likes to drift on his raft and fish for bass in the river.

SLW 9.17

1. l-i-v-e-r	2. f-r-e-e	3. l-o-v-e-r
4. f-i-n-d	5. a-b-o-v-e	6. f-r-e-s-h
7. f-i-g-h-t	8. g-r-a-v-e	9. f-l-i-p-p-e-r

SLW 10.6

1. low	2. rope	3. soap
4. corn	5. store	6. show
7. hope	8. grow	9. fork

10. Grover rowed the old boat to the shore.

SLW 10.11

1. taught	2. law	3. call
4. war	5. ought to	6. cost
7. fraud	8. fall	9. long

10. Paul saw the lost dog with the bad paw.

SLW 10.14

1. w-a-s-h	2. t-a-l-l	3. l-a-w-y-e-r
4. s-h-o-w	5. w-a-r-m	6. t-h-r-o-w
7. s-a-w	8. w-a-l-k	9. t-h-o-u-g-h-t

SLW 11. 6

1. joke	2. age	3. budge
4. jet	5. fridge	6. just
7. stage	8. judge	9. gender

10. Jed and Jill just joined a German class at Jackson State College.

SLW 11.14

1. clue	2. tooth	3. new
4. blew	5. tool	6. stew
7. true	8. boot	9. fruit

10. The pool rule is don't be a fool in the pool. It's not cool.

SLW 11.16

1. a-g-e	2. j-a-m	3. j-o-k-e
4. j-u-m-p	5. e-d-g-e	6. b-a-d-g-e

SLW 12.6
1. quit
2. quiet
3. squash
4. equal
5. question
6. require
7. quake
8. queen
9. quick
10. Squeaky felt quite queer after eating a quart of squid from Quincy Market.

SLW 12.11
1. now
2. clown
3. mouth
4. brown
5. sour
6. sound
7. found
8. vowel
9. cow
10. Howie knows how to make a great meal with a pound of ground round.

SLW 12.13
1. q-u-i-c-k
2. m-o-u-t-h
3. s-q-u-a-s-h
4. c-l-o-w-n
5. q-u-a-k-e
6. q-u-e-s-t-i-o-n
7. v-o-w-e-l
8. q-u-e-e-n
9. e-q-u-a-l-i-t-y

SLW 13.5
1. oil
2. soy
3. joy
4. boil
5. avoid
6. poison
7. noisy
8. destroyed
9. annoyed
10. The boys are employed at Floyd's Toy Store.

SLW 13.12
1. shirt
2. worm
3. farm
4. work
5. certain
6. park
7. murder
8. cart
9. large
10. Herb looked for words that were verbs, and Bart marked the parts that were hard.

SLW14.9
1. zoo
2. taxi
3. box
4. dizzy
5. mixed
6. jazz
7. axes
8. zoom
9. size
10. The lazy zebra and crazy ox dozed six hours in the breeze.

SLW 14.11
1. z-i-p-p-e-r
2. b-o-x-e-r
3. d-o-z-e-n
4. t-a-x-i
5. c-r-a-z-y
6. m-i-x-e-r

COMMON SOUNDS AND SPELLINGS – VOWELS

SOUNDS   **SPELLINGS**

/iy/	E	EA	EE	E..E	IE	EA.. E	EI
	he	eat	see	here	yield	please	either

/i/	I	I..E
	bit	give

/ey/	A..E	AI	AY	EA	EI
	ate	rain	day	great	eight

/e/	E	EA	A	AI
	get	head	many	said

/ae/	A
	bat

/er/	ER	IR	UR	OR
	her	bird	fur	word

/uh/	A	E	I	O	U	O..E
	ago	the	direct	son	but	some

/ay/	I	I..E	Y	IGH	IE
	hi	five	my	high	pie

SOUNDS   SPELLINGS

/a/	O	A
	not	father

/ow/	OW	OU
	now	out

/u/	U	OO	OU
	put	book	would

/uw/	OO	OU	O	U..E	UE	EW	UI
	boot	you	do	rule	true	new	fruit

/yuw/	U	U..E	EW	EU
	unit	jcute	few	Europe

/o/	O	O..E	OW	OA	OUGH
	no	home	low	boat	though

/oy/	OY	OI
	boy	boil

/aw/	AW	A	AU	O
	law	walk	daughter	long

COMMON SOUNDS AND SPELLINGS – CONSONANTS

SOUNDS   SPELLINGS

SOUNDS	SPELLINGS			
/p/	pepper			
/b/	be	rubber		
/t/	ten	bottle	walked	
/d/	day	middle	lived	
/k/	can	black	key	quit
/g/	go	bigger		
/f/	family	phone	enough	
/v/	very			
/th/	thin			
/TH/	the			
/s/	see	city	glass	
/z/	has	zero		

COMMON SOUNDS AND SPELLINGS – CONSONANTS

SOUND	LETTERS/SPELLING		
/sh/	<u>sh</u>e	ac<u>ti</u>on	<u>s</u>ure
/zh/	plea<u>s</u>ure		
/ch/	mu<u>ch</u>	wa<u>tch</u>	ques<u>ti</u>on
/j/	<u>j</u>ust	hu<u>g</u>e	e<u>dg</u>e
/m/	<u>m</u>eet	su<u>mm</u>er	
/n/	<u>n</u>o	di<u>nn</u>er	<u>kn</u>ow
/ng/	si<u>ng</u>	thi<u>n</u>k	
/l/	<u>l</u>ook	ba<u>ll</u>	
/r/	<u>r</u>ead	<u>wr</u>ite	a<u>rr</u>ive
/h/	<u>h</u>ave	<u>wh</u>o	
/y/	<u>y</u>es		
/w/	<u>w</u>e	q<u>u</u>estion	

Other Pro Lingua Books of Interest

√ **SUPERPHONIC BINGO**. 15 **photocopyable** games following the presentation of sound-letter combinations in *From Sound to Sentence*. Each game has 8 different cards and two incomplete cards.

√ **ENGLISH INTERPLAY: SURVIVING**. An integrated skills text for absolute beginners. Lots of pair and small group work. A variety of activities: exchanges, rituals, operations, games, rhymes. Includes grammar notes, pronunciation practice. Features 10 units focused on survival language. Separate
√ **TEACHER'S BOOK** is available. Includes all the student material plus suggestions and instructions for the teacher and additional resource material.

STRESS RULZ. The rules of stress placement in English are presented as **photocopyable** raps. An accompanying **CD** dramatically captures the rhythm of spoken English in dynamic raps.

RHYMES 'N' RHYTHMS. Your students will enjoy the choral work in these 32 rhythmic rhymes that develop the student's ability to speak with English stress, rhythm, and intonation. A **CD** is also available for use with this **photocopyable** text.

GRANDPARENTS ARE SPECIAL. A high-beginner/low-intermediate reader about an immigrant family. The young ESL student discovers her grandmother is illiterate, and helps her learn to read. A **photocopyable TEACHER'S GUIDE** provides additional material. **Cassette** or **CD** also available.

PRONUNCIATION ACTIVITIES: VOWELS IN LIMERICKS. 16 comical limericks present the basic vowels of English. Each limerick is followed by a variety of pronunciation and sound-letter correspondence activities. **Cassette** or **CD** available.

THE INTERACTIVE TUTORIAL. 57 **photocopyable** activities for adult learners, beginning to low intermediate level. Designed for one-on-one tutoring, but easily adaptable for use with small groups.

THE READ AND LEARN SERIES. Four separate, graded readers. In **READ 50**, the average passage is only 50 words long. The other books are **READ 75**, **READ 100**, and **READ 125**. Each reading passage is followed with brief exercises. A wide variety of topics and formats are included in the 160 passages in the four-book collection. **CD**s are available.

Pro Lingua Associates

P.O. Box 1348

Brattleboro, VT 05302

Orders: (800) 366-4775

FAX: (802) 257-5117

Email: Info@ProLinguaAssociates.com

Web Store: www.ProLinguaAssociates.com